When Life Is a ZOO God Still Loves You

BOB RUSSELL

STANDARD
PUBLISHING
Cincinnati, Ohio

Unless otherwise noted, all Scripture references are from the Holy Bible: New International Version, ©1973, 1978, 1984 by the International Bible Society. Used by permission of Zondervan Bible Publishers. All rights reserved.

The "NIV" and "New International Version" trademarks are registered in the United States Patent Office by International Bible Society. Use of either trademark requires the permission of International Bible Society.

Library of Congress Cataloging-in-Publication data:

Russell, Bob, 1943-

When life is a zoo, God still loves you / Bob Russell.
   p. cm.
ISBN 0-7847-0078-8
1. Animals in the Bible.   2. Animals--Religious aspects--Christianity. I. Title
BS663.R87   1992
220.8'591--dc20   92-39186
                                                          CIP

The Standard Publishing Company, Cincinnati, Ohio.
A division of Standex International Corporation.

99 98 97 96 95 94 93 92   5 4 3 2 1

Contents

Preface

This book is a refreshing change of pace from heavily theological and exegetical studies. While thoroughly biblical, this book is topical in nature. It looks at some familiar events in biblical history from the interesting perspective of the animals involved.

No attempt is made to spiritualize the events. The author believes each event to be a true historical incedent. Yet there is more than history here. The record of God's dealings with his creation—both human and animal—provides fascinating lessons for Christians today.

This book may be used in a variety of settings. Many people will simply enjoy sitting down and reading it. Some will read it cover to cover in one setting. Others may enjoy reading a chapter or two each evening while they unwind from the hectic day's pace.

With the available leader's guide, some Sunday school classes will want to use it for a quarter of study. Vacation Bible Schools may use five or ten of the lessons for youth or adult courses. (Standard Publishing's 1993 VBS course is closely coordinated with this study.) Midweek study groups will also find the lessons stimulating and a refreshing change, perhaps, from straight verse-by-verse type of studies.

The animal kingdom is a delightful illustration of the creativity and loving care of God. Not even a sparrow falls, Jesus said, without the Father's taking note. His care for human beings is even more intense, for God is not willing that any should perish, but that all should come to repentance and find life in his Son. Of all the creatures God has made, the crown of creation is humanity, men and women, whom God loves and for whom he wants only the best.

A Biblical View of Animals

Psalm 104

I grew up on a farm. Cows, chickens, dogs, cats, pigs, horses, mules, and sheep were a part of my childhood experiences. I can remember watching my father shoot rats that were robbing the corn crib. I remember scaring my sisters with the black snakes I had caught. I remember milking cows, butchering pigs, collecting eggs, and hunting rabbits. I remember watching puppies open their eyes for the first time.

I was recently privileged to take a two-week tour of Kenya, Africa. It was quite a thrill to see giraffes, ostriches, wildebeast, zebras, hippos, elands, monkeys, warthogs, buffalo, tropical birds, and other animals in their natural surroundings. My heart skipped a beat or two when a rhinoceros confronted our four-wheel-drive vehicle and seemed to contemplate charging. We were thankful he decided to leave us alone! Seeing all these creatures up close was not only exciting, it deepened my appreciation for the variety of God's creation.

I believe Christians should hold a special appreciation for the animals because the Bible tells us in Genesis 1 that God created the heavens and the earth, including the "living creatures."

One can learn a lot about a person by examining the product he or she creates. Reading a book reveals a lot about the author. Viewing a painting reveals the heart of the painter. A musical composition tells something about the composer. You can even pass by a front lawn and discern things about the owner of that property.

The same is true with the God of the universe. While we learn about God primarily through the Bible, his Word, we can also study his character by observing the things that he has created.

Psalm 104:24 declares: "How many are your works, O Lord! In wisdom you made them all; the earth is full of your creatures."

This book is a study of some of the animals of the Bible. You will be intrigued, entertained, and moved by these true stories that focus on God's creatures. But our primary purpose in studying the animals is to gain insight into the character of their Creator. We will see afresh that God still loves us even when our lives are complex and imperfect.

Before you begin, you must understand four important Biblical principles concerning animals. First, animals belong to God and should, therefore, be respected and loved. Second, animals were created by God to be inferior to man. They are not to be revered or worshiped. Third, animals are for the benefit of man, and should be used and appreciated. Finally, animals can teach us some valuable spiritual lessons.

Animals Belong to God

When you see a watch, you know there has to be a watch maker. How can someone study the complex design of the animals and not be convinced that there must be a Master Designer?

I understand that a kangaroo at birth is not much bigger than a dime. When that tiny kangaroo is dropped from the womb, it instinctively climbs up its mother's coat, crawls inside her protective pouch, and lives there for several weeks until it is mature enough to survive on its own. How could that survival instinct possibly evolve by accident? Could a tiny kangaroo, that would die if left to itself, communicate to generations not yet born that if they wanted to survive they must find a special pouch several feet away from the place where they entered the world? How could a mother kangaroo instruct her body to grow that special protective pouch? There is only one logical explanation: "In the beginning God created the heavens and the earth" (Genesis 1:1).

We've all heard the expression "blind as a bat." The expression is well-founded. A bat has such poor eyesight that it can barely discern light from darkness. Yet a bat can fly into a dark cave and easily maneuver through tunnels and around stalactites by using its own sonar system. The bat sends out a high-pitched chirp that is almost inaudible. The sound's frequency is so high that it even detects small insects the bat may be capturing for food. The relatively large ears of the bat allow it to hear the frequency and navigate swiftly—even in total darkness. It took centuries for man to discover sonar, but bats have been using it from the beginning of time.

Let's consider the migration of birds. A chimney swift is a small swallow commonly seen flying on summer nights. In late summer, all the chimney swifts suddenly disappear. For years, experts knew they migrated, but no one knew where they were going. Ornithologists finally began banding the little birds to find out. They discovered the birds were wintering in Peru and returning to the same area every summer. I have a hard time finding my way to Florida with a road map on super highways. That bird goes to South America, with no roads or maps, and finds its way back to the same birdhouse in your back yard every year.

The humming bird, the smallest of all birds, flies from as far north as Maine to the Gulf Coast for winter. Some humming birds fly 500 miles across the open waters of the Gulf of Mexico into South America!

One of the most amazing of all birds is the golden plover. It nests in the tundra of Alaska and Canada and winters in Central America. That's a long trip. When a golden plover migrates south, it takes a route along the east coast into South America. But its return trip north involves a westward route across the Gulf of Mexico, into the Mississippi valley, and through the central United States. The round trip is over 15,000 miles!

The Scripture is true: "The glory of the Lord fills the whole earth" (Numbers 14:21). Psalm 50:10 reads, "For every animal of the forest is mine, and the cattle on a thousand hills." If these amazing creatures belong to God, then they deserve our love and respect.

If your grandfather gave you a special piece of furniture that he had made, your care for that piece would reflect your love for your grandfather. In a similar way, God created the animals and gave them to man. Our treatment of the animals reflects our respect for God.

We know that Adam took the time to give every animal a distinctive name. Noah spent 120 years building enough space on the ark to preserve each species. God expects us to be faithful stewards of the animal kingdom entrusted to our care. A person who neglects to feed or provide properly for his pets reveals a lack of appreciation for the Creator. Someone who kills or hurts animals without purpose reveals a sinister spirit and is disrespectful to the God who owns the earth.

11

William Wilberforce took a public stand against cruelty to animals in the 1800s. His stance was not in the name of animal rights but in the name of Christian stewardship. "A righteous man cares for the needs of his animal, but the kindest acts of the wicked are cruel" (Proverbs 12:10).

Animals Are Inferior to Humans

The second biblical principle is this: animals were created by God to be inferior to people. They are not to be revered or worshiped.

If one wants to insult another person, he might compare that person to an animal. To label someone a pig, a turkey, a dog, an elephant, a mouse, a rat, or a snake is not complimentary. In the same way, to make an image of an animal and call it "God" is a gross insult to the Heavenly Father. Yet the idols of many ancient cultures were made to look like the beasts of the field and the birds of the air.

In the book of Exodus, the Hebrew people, who had received a special revelation from Jehovah only a few weeks before, fashioned a golden calf and worshiped it as God. They said to one another, "These are your gods, O Israel, who brought you up out of Egypt" (Exodus 32:4). Their false worship angered God so much that He executed three thousand of the guilty. There are religions even today that are guilty of degrading God by worshiping animals. Starvation is rampant in many Hindu cultures. There would be plenty of beef available, but they refuse to kill their cattle for food because, in the mind of the Hindu, a cow is something to be worshiped.

Paul wrote:

For although they knew God, they neither glorified him as God nor gave thanks to him, but their thinking became futile and their foolish hearts were darkened. Although they claimed to be wise, they became fools and exchanged the glory of the immortal God for images made to look like mortal man and birds and animals and reptiles (Romans 1:21-23).

The Bible teaches that animals have value, but the Scriptures warn us repeatedly that animals are not to be worshiped. Nor are they to be considered to be as valuable as a human life.

Some will try to suggest that the lives of animals are as valuable as the lives of humans. The idea that man is not superior to animals was illustrated graphically in a recent advertisement

12

by a group called "People for the Ethical Treatment of Animals." The advertisement compared the slaughter of cows and chickens for food to the mass murders committed by Jeffrey Dahlmer—as if killing animals and killing humans were moral equivalents. The Bible would not support those who insist that the animals are as valuable as humans and entitled to the same protection. When animals are given too much value, the result is that human life is devalued. Here are some examples:

Much effort is being expended to protect the spotted owl in the Oregon forest, though hundreds of lumbermen are being forced out of work.

Some environmentalists have gone to extremes in protecting wetlands, though their efforts have brought unreasonable hardships to communities, churches, and families.

Many are spending incredible amounts of energy and money to save whales in Alaska, but they turn their heads when millions of babies are aborted.

In contrast, Genesis 1:27 reads, "So God created man in his own image, in the image of God he created him; male and female he created them." The Bible says that man is the highest of God's physical creation. Man alone was created in the image of God. It was man whom Christ loved enough to die for, that we might live with him for eternity.

Charles Colson wrote, "The animal-rights movement is not just about being kind to animals. It's about a radically naturalistic worldview that denies any special status to humans. Animal rights promises a naturalistic utopia, where we live in harmony with nature. But this is a secular substitute for heaven, where, instead of Christ coming down to earth, humanity comes down to the level of animals." He cites Ingrid Newkirk, president of People for the Ethical Treatment of Animals, who said. "A rat is a pig is a dog is a boy!"[1]

Twenty-six years ago, when my wife and I were first married, we saw evidence of a mouse in our house, so I set a mousetrap. In the middle of the night I awakened and heard an intruder on our basement steps. Sometimes in those situations, you think you might have heard something, but you're not certain. I was certain! It was unmistakable. What I didn't know was that my mousetrap had been tripped. But the mouse that tripped it was so small that the trap caught only its tail. That

---

[1]Charles Colson, *The Body* (Dallas: Word, Inc., 1992). Used by permission.

tiny mouse had dragged the trap across the kitchen floor and had slipped under the door leading to the basement. From the bedroom, I could hear the clapping of that mousetrap as it hit each step descending to the basement! My heart leaped to my throat. I was newly married and was determined to protect my wife. I had no weapon, so I grabbed the lamp beside the bed. I was nearly hyperventilating, but I managed to tiptoe to the basement door. I stood to the side, flung open the door, and shouted in a trembling voice, "All right, come on out of there!"

I peered around the corner and saw that tiny mouse about five steps down. I must have looked like Barney Fife when I turned to my wife and said, "It's only a mouse. I figured as much."

I told that story to the church where I was preaching, and a twelve-year-old boy approached me after the sermon. He said, "Brother Bob, what did you do with that mouse?"

I said, "I took it outside and drowned it in a bucket of water as fast as I could."

That young man loved all animals—even mice! By the look on his face, I could tell he was devastated that his preacher would kill one of God's creatures. That is an understandable childish reaction. From a mature and Scriptural viewpoint, I did nothing wrong by defending my wife and killing that mouse.

The fifth chapter of Mark tells of Jesus' encounter with a man who was possessed by a legion of demons. When Jesus ordered the demons to release the man and come out, they begged him to send them into a nearby herd of pigs. When Jesus honored their request, the entire herd of two thousand pigs rushed down a steep bank and drowned themselves in a lake. Jesus allowed two thousand pigs to be destroyed to show that the soul of one man had supreme value.

Jesus said, "What good will it be for a man if he gains the whole world, yet forfeits his soul?" (Matthew 16:26).

Animals Are for People's Benefit

God himself ordained the use of animals to provide for people's physical needs, like food and clothing. When Adam and Eve sinned, they made fig leaves for themselves to hide their nakedness. But fig leaves were insufficient, so God made them garments of animal skin (Genesis 3:6-21).

The Bible does not teach that it is sinful to wear a garment of animal skins or furs. John the Baptist was described by Jesus as the greatest man born to woman, and he wore a garment of camel skin and girded himself with a leather belt. To protest against the wearing of fur coats, leather shoes, or coonskin caps is not a sign of spirituality. It reveals a lack of appreciation for the uniqueness of man and the authorization God has given for the utilization of his creation.

God also made it clear after the flood that animals were given to man for food: "*Everything* that lives and moves will be food for you. Just as I gave you green plants I now give you everything. But you must not eat meat that has its lifeblood still in it" (Genesis 9:3, 4). Noah and his descendants were given permission to eat meat that was properly prepared.

In Mark 7:19, Jesus declared all foods to be "clean." Jesus himself ate fish and the meat of the passover lamb (Luke 22:7, 8; 24:42). In a parable, he spoke of a father who celebrated his son's return by killing and eating a fatted calf (Luke 15:23).

We are given permission to eat steak, fish, chicken, pork, and any other meat that is properly cooked. Some might argue that a vegetarian is healthier, but a meatless diet is not an indication of spirituality. God intended for animals to be used to meet human needs.

Animals Can Teach Us Valuable Spiritual Lessons

This book will examine some Biblical examples of how God used animals to teach his people valuable spiritual lessons. A donkey, a rooster, a lamb, a fish, lions, birds and other animals were used in the Bible to illustrate important truths about God's relationship with man.

But even today one can be reminded of spiritual truths by observing the animals. One day recently I looked out my office window and watched an exciting drama unfold on the front yard of the church. One of the ladies in our church, Karen Bakken, had stopped her car and was watching a mother duck lead seven tiny baby ducklings down the driveway. The mother duck hopped over the curb and started across the lawn, but only one of the little ducklings could get over the curb on its own. The others seemed hopelessly trapped by the curb. The mother kept waddling along the curb toward the street, trying to persuade her little ones to jump over the curb, but they couldn't do it.

Karen could see that if something didn't happen, the baby ducks would waddle right into the busy street. Being an animal lover, she took action. She quickly got into her car and pulled it across the entrance, then jumped out to assist the ducklings. But by that time, one of them had fallen through a grate into the sewer. She lifted all the others up over the curb and directed them toward the anxious mother just a few feet away. The mother duck took off with her six little ones hurrying behind.

But now there was a duckling in the sewer. Karen peered down into the sewer but could not possibly reach the panicking duckling. She started sadly for her car, then turned back and looked again. She tried to leave, but couldn't bring herself to abandon the little duckling to die in the sewer.

Just then I saw three men coming down the walk, and I knew what was going to happen. I had foreknowledge! Karen called to the three men to assist her. One of them lifted off the grate, climbed down into the sewer and disappeared. Moments later he handed up a little duckling and climbed out of the sewer. Karen thanked the men as they walked away.

Karen was then left with a baby duck and no mother. The mother duck was long gone. I last saw Karen getting into her car and driving off with that little duckling in search of the mother duck.

Jesus said, "Look at the birds of the air; they do not sow or reap or store away in barns, and yet your heavenly Father feeds them. Are you not much more valuable than they?" (Matthew 6:26).

If we as humans can become so distraught over a little bird lost in the sewer, how much more difficult it must be for God to bear the thought of one of us being lost and alienated from him.

All of us have fallen into sin. As a result, we are alienated from God and hopelessly lost. But God in His infinite love, came down into the sewer of this world in the form of Jesus Christ to save us. He alone can lift us out of the mire of sin and set us on higher ground. He alone can restore us to a right relationship with our Creator.

Karen Bakken's concern for those ducks illustrated again for me God's infinite love for man. I decided later to use that incident as a sermon illustration and called Karen to make sure I had the details of the story correct. She said there was something I had missed. There was not just one little duckling in the sewer. Two others had fallen through the grate, but the man who had rescued the one couldn't reach the other two. He said, "I called to them, but they would not come."

When Jesus knew his final days were nearing, he stood over the city of Jerusalem and wept. He said, "O Jerusalem,

Jerusalem, . . . how often I have longed to gather your children together, as a hen gathers her chicks under her wings, but you were not willing" (Matthew 23:37).

Jesus came to earth to save us. He calls, "Come unto me, and I will give you rest," and, "Whosoever will may come." But sadly, not everyone responds to His offer of salvation. Some resist because of fear, ignorance, stubbornness, or a misguided sense of freedom. But only those who are willing to come to Jesus Christ and submit to His nail-pierced hands will be saved.

The animals are fascinating creatures, and they provide for an intriguing study. Throughout this book, the reader will do well to remember: Animals should be respected as part of God's creation, and they can teach us some valuable spiritual lessons. But they should never be considered to be as valuable in the eyes of God as one human soul. "Of all God's creatures great and small, God loves you best of all."

CHAPTER 1

The Ark Parade

Genesis 6–9

God saw how corrupt the earth had become, for all the people on earth had corrupted their ways. So God said to Noah, "I am going to put an end to all people, for the earth is filled with violence because of them. I am surely going to destroy both them and the earth. So make yourself an ark of cypress wood; make rooms in it and coat it with pitch inside and out. . . . Two of every kind of bird, of every kind of animal and of every kind of creature that moves along the ground will come to you to be kept alive" (Genesis 6:12-14, 20).

Our community was stunned recently by the brutal murder of a twelve-year-old girl. Jealous of the younger girl's influence over a mutual girlfriend, a sixteen-year-old girl enticed her into a car, held her at knife point, beat her with a blunt object, strangled her, and threw her into the trunk of the car. She later doused her body with gasoline and burned her to death.

We shudder at stories like that. What are we to conclude about the condition of our world when a teenaged girl could be so depraved? Jesus said in, "As it was in the days of Noah, so it will be at the coming of the Son of Man" (Matthew 24:37).

The Lord saw how great man's wickedness on the earth had become, and that every inclination of the thoughts of his heart was only evil all the time. The Lord was grieved that he had made man on the earth, and his heart was filled with pain. So the Lord said, "I will wipe mankind, whom I have created, from the face of the earth—men and animals, and creatures that move along the ground, and the birds of the air—for I am grieved that I have made them" (Genesis 6:5-7).

Much like people today, people in Noah's day weren't very concerned about God. They were totally absorbed in selfish pursuits. They were concerned only about lust, greed, power, and pleasure.

Man's preoccupation with himself incurred the wrath of God, and the whole earth was about to be destroyed, including the animals. Even God's creatures must suffer the consequences of man's sins.

But there was one righteous man whom God was going to use to save a remnant of both man and the animals. "Noah found favor in the eyes of the Lord" (Genesis 6:8). In today's corrupt and violent world, it is comforting to be reminded that God is still in control and still provides for his people. The familiar story of Noah and the ark will demonstrate to the reader that God used animals to provide for man's needs even when man was at his worst.

A Warning of Impending Judgment

God's creatures provided one last dramatic warning that the world was going to be destroyed.

God came to Noah and told him to build a huge ship to prepare for a world-wide flood. As far as we can tell, Noah had never even seen it rain! (Genesis 2:5). But Noah was a "righteous man, blameless among the people of his time, and he walked with God" (Genesis 6:9). If God said there was going to be judgment, he believed it. If God said, "Construct an ark," he would build an ark.

Noah went to work building an ocean liner in the middle of a field. It had to be a major tourist attraction! There were probably signs on barns that advertised, "See Noah's ark, five miles!" For 120 years Noah constructed the ark, endured the cruel jokes, and pleaded with people to repent, but nobody believed him. Noah could not win one convert outside of his own family.

People must have asked Noah why he was constructing hundreds of compartments inside the ark. When he informed them he was building stalls and cages so all the animals could be saved from the coming flood, he must have been ridiculed unmercifully! But God used the animals to provide one final spectacular warning to man.

God had instructed Noah to take a male and female of each kind of animal onto the ark (Genesis 6:19). It would have been impossible for Noah to roam the earth, capture a male and female of every creature, and keep them all alive while he constructed the ark. But Noah didn't have to corral the animals. One week before the flood, an extraordinary event unfolded: the wild animals began parading to the ark! They came to Noah instinctively. They came at God's direction: "Pairs of clean and unclean animals, of birds and of all creatures that move along the ground, male and female, came to Noah and entered the ark" (Genesis 7:8, 9).

Noah's critics had to have been impressed when hundreds of wild animals marched voluntarily into the ark. Predator and prey were walking through the door together. Animals that would be expected to run in fear, or strike out in defense, entered the ark and went to their designated places without resistance. People had never seen anything like it! The animal parade must have been the topic of conversation throughout the entire community. Even the most intellectual skeptic could not offer a reasonable explanation.

That miraculous migration of animals should have proven to the world that Noah's claim of divine instruction was true. It was God's final warning to repent and flee to the ark for safety. But no one heeded the warning.

Jesus said:

> In the days before the flood, people were eating and drinking, marrying and giving in marriage, up to the day Noah entered the ark; and they knew nothing about what would happen until the flood came and took them all away. That is how it will be at the coming of the Son of Man (Matthew 24:38, 39).

Noah had been preaching for 120 years. The animals had paraded miraculously into the ark. But despite all those warnings from God, the people still "knew nothing about what would happen" because their hearts were hard and their ears were deadened. They were too preoccupied with their own selfish pursuits to consider the possibility that Noah's warning could be true.

Jesus warned that the same attitudes would prevail in the day of the coming of the Son of Man. People will continue in their selfish pursuits, ignoring the warnings of ministers and the signs of the times, until the Son of Man comes and it is too late.

A Stimulus to Meaningful Labor

For Noah and his family, God's creatures provided a stimulus to meaningful labor. Building the ark and caring for the animals had to be hard work! Henry Morris says there are less than 18,000 species of animals today. Through fossil records, it is apparent that many animals have become extinct since Noah's day, so Morris estimates that 36,000 species of animals were parading to the ark. They came in pairs, which would make 72,000 animals. When one allows for the additional clean animals Noah was commanded to take, it can be estimated that there were 75,000 animals on Noah's ark! The ark was about 1,400,000 cubic feet, which equals the capacity of 522 standard livestock railroad cars. Sixty percent of the ark's capacity would be needed just to house the animals.[2] It's no wonder Noah and his sons worked for 120 years building the ark!

Noah was a lumberjack, a shipbuilder, and a carpenter, and then he became a zookeeper. Ask any mother whose husband thought it would be nice to give the children a pet for Christmas, and she will tell you that caring for an animal takes work. Whether it is a rabbit, dog, cat, gerbil, bird, or pet snake, someone has to feed, groom, train, and clean up after that new pet. Noah was responsible for a zoo full of animals.

God commanded Noah, "You are to take every kind of food that is to be eaten and store it away as food for you and for them" (Genesis 6:21).

Noah had to build stables and granaries. He had to haul hay, wheat, and straw. He had to prepare to feed and care for 75,000 animals. The only thing he didn't have to store was water—there would be plenty of that! Once they entered the ark, the animals had to be fed, manure had to be hauled, straw needed to be redistributed, and cows had to be milked. But Noah's work was a blessing.

Many people think that work is a curse we suffer because of sin. But work was part of man's perfect existence in the Garden of Eden. The curse was not that man would have to work, but that he would have to deal with soil that wouldn't cooperate. Work is a blessing, and idleness is a curse. David Jacobson, an American who was held hostage in Lebanon for seventeen months, said that one of the most difficult things about being a hostage was having to live in a small room with absolutely

[2]Henry Morris, *The Genesis Record* (Grand Rapids: Baker Book House, 1976), pages 181, 185.

nothing to do for days. One of the worst curses in the world is to have nothing to do.

Noah and his family were on the ark for over a year. If they had been by themselves with nothing to do, they would have been bored to tears, and their boredom would have led to depression. But they did not have time to get bored or depressed. Taking care of that floating zoo kept them occupied. Man never feels better about himself than when he feels he has accomplished something useful. Noah and his family worked hard, but they knew they were accomplishing something useful by helping God save the animals.

Companionship for Lonely People

In the Garden of Eden, Adam was given the assignment to name all of the animals. As the animals passed in front of Adam, he gave each one a specific name. "But for Adam, no suitable helper was found" (Genesis 2:20). God wanted Adam to know that no animal can satisfy man's deep longing for communication, understanding and fellowship. But animals can provide a certain degree of companionship for lonely people. The animals on the ark must have provided companionship for the sequestered people on board.

Therapists often recommend that lonely people get pets to keep them company. Many people admit their animals have comforted them in difficult times.

Hillary McGee, a member of our church, purchased a pet pig for her husband Bill one Christmas. It seems odd to have a pig for a pet, but Bill insists that his pig is smarter than any dog he has ever seen. When his neighbors find out he has a pet pig, he'll need the companionship!

Mike Bayer of our church went through a period of depression when his wife was murdered years ago. He told me that during those times he was reminded of the slogan, "The more I know of men, the more I like my dogs."

Mike said, "I would pull the van in back of the house so no one would know I was home. I would go down to the lower level of the house, unplug the telephone, and go into mourning for days." His only companions were his two akita dogs. Mike said, "During that period, my dogs were all I had. I would talk to them, get angry at them, feed them or ignore them, and they loved me just the same. They were the only thing I could count on. I really feel God used those animals and their unconditional love to keep me going at a time when I could barely survive. It was a time in my life when I needed something consistent regardless of how I felt."

Tom Morgard, a friend of mine in Pennsylvania, said that when he was notified of his father's death, he lay on the couch and sobbed. His cocker spaniel crawled up onto his chest. Tom said, "I know that my dog sensed something was wrong. He reached up and licked away the tears on my face."

When I was younger, I was especially close to one pet, a dog named Kip. I will never forget the hurt that I felt when Kip was hit by an automobile and died.

Animals can provide a certain degree of companionship for people. Although Noah probably got frustrated with the animals on the ark, I suspect he learned to love and appreciate them as well.

A Revelation of the Earth's Condition

Noah was on the ark for a long time. It rained for forty days and forty nights, but it took much longer for the waters to recede from the earth.

People sometimes complain about "cabin fever" when they are confined to the house for a period of time. When a snowstorm prevents a family from leaving the house for days, family members may get on each other's nerves, feel restricted, and become depressed. "I just need to get out," they'll say. One can only imagine the "cabin fever" that Noah and his family must have experienced when confined to the ark for months!

It was over five months before the ark came to rest on Mount Ararat (Genesis 7:24; 8:3, 4). But Noah and his family could not immediately leave the ark. They had to wait for the waters to recede, the mud to dry up, and vegetation to begin growing so that the animals could live again on their own. "But God remembered Noah and all the wild animals and the livestock that were with him in the ark, and he sent a wind over the earth and the waters receded" (Genesis 8:1).

Still, it took another two and a half months just for the tops of the mountains to become visible (Genesis 8:5). Noah's patience must have been tested. It could not have been pleasant to be confined to that smelly boat with no idea how much longer they would be in there.

Apparently, Noah could not conclude much by looking out of the ark's only window. Perhaps the window was facing the wall of a cliff. Noah needed to determine the condition of the earth, so he decided to use two of the birds he had cared for on the ark. "After forty days Noah opened the window he had made in the ark and sent out a raven, and it kept flying back and forth until the water dried up from the earth" (Genesis 8:6, 7).

The raven is a scavenger and would have no qualms about resting on unclean surfaces. It would have been the first creature to survive outside the ark. The raven must have discovered enough dead fish and food outside the ark to sustain itself, because it did not return to the ark.

So Noah performed another experiment. He sent out a dove to see if the water had receded from the ground.

But the dove could find no place to set its feet because there was water over all the surface of the earth; so it returned to Noah in the ark. He reached out his hand and took the dove and brought it back to himself in the ark (Genesis 8:9).

A week later, Noah sent out the dove again. This time it returned with a fresh olive leaf in its beak. Noah then knew that the seedlings from the hardy olive trees were already beginning to grow on the mountainside. "He waited seven more days and sent the dove out again, but this time it did not return to him" (Genesis 8:12).

Noah now knew that the land was dry enough to support bird life. He waited about another month before he removed the covering from the ark and looked at the surface of the ground. But Noah must have concluded that the land was still too barren to sustain the lives of most of the animals, because he waited another fifty-seven days before he exited the ark.

Then God said to Noah, "Come out of the ark, you and your wife and your sons and their wives. Bring out every kind of living creature that is with you—the birds, the animals, and all the creatures that move along the ground—so they can multiply on the earth and be fruitful and increase in number upon it" (Genesis 8:15, 16).

It was a long ordeal. Noah and his family were actually in the ark over a year—371 days altogether! But the dove and the raven had helped reveal the condition of the earth while Noah waited.

One of the controversies that troubles people today is the use of animals in experimentation. Is it right to use guinea pigs, rabbits, monkeys, and rats in laboratory experiments? Should people allow animals to be afflicted with diseases in order to benefit mankind in the future?

I think the answer is yes—at least in some cases. Noah risked the lives of a raven and a dove in an experiment to see whether the ground could support the rest of the animals and his family. Animals should never be tortured, neglected, or abused, nor should they be killed without purpose. But animals exist for the benefit of man. Animals should be respected as God's creatures, but the Bible makes it clear that man is to be viewed as God's highest creation.

> Then God blessed Noah and his sons, saying to them, "Be fruitful and increase in number and fill the earth. The fear and dread of you will fall upon all the beasts of the earth and all the birds of the air, upon every creature that moves along the ground, and upon all the fish of the sea; they are given into your hands" (Genesis 9:1, 2).

If one human life is spared at the expense of an animal, then the purpose of the animal has been fulfilled. Jesus allowed the health of one man to take precedence over the lives of two thousand pigs (Mark 5:1-20). Jesus was not degrading the value of animals, but acknowledging the value of one human life.

A Prototype of Man's Salvation

Noah, his family, and all the animals were finally able to exit the ark. The first thing Noah did when he disembarked (after he kissed the ground, I'm sure!) was to put to death some of the animals and to offer them as a sacrifice to God.

> Then Noah built an altar to the Lord and, taking some of all the clean animals and clean birds, he sacrificed burnt offerings on it. The Lord smelled the pleasing aroma and said in his heart: "Never again will I curse the ground because of man, even though every inclination of his heart is evil from childhood. And never again will I destroy all living creatures, as I have done" (Genesis 8:20, 21).

The animal sacrifice was pleasing to the Lord. God had commanded Noah to take onto the ark two of all the unclean animals, and seven of all the clean animals, so that some could be used for sacrifices. Noah sacrificed some of the animals out of obedience and thanksgiving to the Lord.

God required animal sacrifices throughout the Old Testament. His purpose was not to cheapen the value of animals, but to demonstrate the costliness of man's sin. When Adam and Eve sinned in the Garden of Eden, God killed an animal and made them garments of skin. It was a lesson to them that sin could not be covered without the shedding of blood (Genesis 3:21).

But the Old Testament sacrifices were only prototypes of a sacrifice to come. God was pleased when a lamb was sacrificed according to his instructions, but an animal could not really take away sin. Hebrews 10:4 reminds us, "It is impossible for the blood of bulls and goats to take away sins." Those sacrifices were object lessons—reminders that man's sins could only be pardoned through the blood of one ultimate human sacrifice.

The Jewish people were able to understand the meaning of Jesus' sacrifice on the cross because hundreds of thousands of God's creatures had given their lives as object lessons. Those animals had died as prototypes, to prepare the way for the One who would die once for all. That is the reason John the Baptist, when he saw Jesus, said, "Look, the Lamb of God, who takes away the sin of the world!" (John 1:29).

CHAPTER 2

God Will Take Care of You

1 Kings 17:1-6

My wife Judy and I began dating when I was a freshman in college. On our third date we went to see a new Alfred Hitchcock movie, *The Birds*. If you have seen the movie, you will no doubt remember that it features a massive rebellion on the part of every kind of bird imaginable. Hundreds of thousands of birds gather in imposing flocks and ferociously attack unsuspecting human beings.

The theater was packed when we arrived, and the only two seats available were on the front row. We sat right beneath the screen for ninety horrifying minutes, looking up at those huge, violent birds as they savagely pecked through houses and automobiles to devour their terrified prey. As the movie grew in intensity, so did Judy's grip on my arm. I may owe my marriage to Alfred Hitchcock's *The Birds!* To this day, when we see birds flocking together, we still laugh about our experiences during that movie.

In 1 Kings 17, there is a true story about some birds who reacted in a strange way. Like Alfred Hitchcock's birds, they did something contrary to their nature, but they didn't attack— they shared. Instead of destroying, they saved.

The prophet Elijah owed his life to the unusual behavior of a flock of ravens. Let's study the account and learn some valuable lessons from the birds.

A Drought Predicted

Now Elijah the Tishbite, from Tishbe in Gilead, said to Ahab, "As the Lord, the God of Israel, lives, whom I serve, there will be neither dew nor rain in the next few years except at my word" (1 Kings 17:1).

29

So reads the Bible's introduction to the prophet Elijah. He steps onto the scene rather abruptly, "like a flash of lightning at midnight," as J. Vernon McGee put it.

Though almost no information regarding his birth or background is provided, Elijah becomes one of the most important men in the Old Testament. Elijah made his mark in history by standing boldly for the truth and performing several spectacular miracles to prove his authority. He was a rugged, courageous individualist, much like John the Baptist in the New Testament.

The story's antagonist is King Ahab, who, in sharp contrast to Elijah, was one of the most wicked rulers in Israel's history. He reigned as the champion of evil for twenty-two years, leading Israel to a level of immorality that saw thousands of babies sacrificed to false gods. "Ahab son of Omri did more evil in the eyes of the Lord than any of those before him" (1 Kings 16:30).

You will hear people say, "Well, I had a tryst a few years ago, but every marriage has problems. Everybody has an affair once in a while."

Ahab had that kind of spirit toward idol worship. "He . . . considered it trivial to commit the sins of Jeroboam . . ." (1 Kings 16:31). "Oh, it's kind of the in thing these days," he was saying. "All the other nations are doing it. After all, it's 870 B.C.!"

That's not the worst of his crimes. "he also married Jezebel daughter of Ethbaal king of the Sidonians, and began to serve Baal and worship him" (1 Kings 16:31).

When Ahab married Jezebel, a seedbed of evil was planted. It was as if Ozzie Osborne had decided to marry Madonna. It was an unholy union.

> He set up an altar for Baal in the temple of Baal that he built in Samaria. Ahab also made an Asherah pole and did more to provoke the Lord, the God of Israel, to anger than did all the kings of Israel before him (1 Kings 16:32, 33).

An Asherah pole was a wooden idol of the Canaanite goddess Asherah, believed to be the consort of Baal. "Worship" of this goddess included prostitution, and was frequently linked to Baal worship. Ahab succeeded in elevating the worship of Baal to an official status in Israel. What had been illegal and an abomination became approved and encouraged.

It is not surprising that Elijah was sent to pronounce judgment on the land. God's patience had run out, and a time of wrath had come. Elijah, in his debut performance, prophesied that a severe famine would cripple Israel for years. Elijah told Ahab, "There will be neither dew nor rain in the next few years except at my word" (1 Kings 17:1).

Elijah gave a bad weather report. The drought that followed was no fluke of nature, but a deliberate act of judgment from God.

In Deuteronomy, Moses had prophesied that, if the Israelites obeyed the Lord, they would be blessed, but if they disobeyed, they would be cursed. Individuals are judged after they die, but how does God judge a nation? He cannot reward or punish a nation after it ceases to exist, so God judges nations here on earth. Moses wrote:

> The Lord will open the heavens, the storehouse of his bounty, to send rain on your land in season and to bless all the work of your hands. You will lend to many nations but will borrow from none. The Lord will make you the head, not the tail. If you pay attention to the commands of the Lord your God that I give you this day and carefully follow them, you will always be at the top, never at the bottom. . . .
>
> However, if you do not obey the Lord your God and do not carefully follow all his commands and decrees I am giving you today, all these curses will come upon you and overtake you. . . .
> The sky over your head will be bronze, the ground beneath you iron. The Lord will turn the rain of your country into dust and powder; it will come down from the skies until you are destroyed (Deuteronomy 28:12, 13, 15, 23, 24).

For the disobedient nation, God promised there would be weather patterns that would vacillate between droughts and destructive floods. Moses continued:

> The alien who lives among you will rise above you higher and higher, but you will sink lower and lower. He will lend to you, but you will not lend to him. He will be the head, but you will be the tail (Deuteronomy 28:43, 44)

According to God's promise, a disobedient nation would cease to be a world leader, and there would be a trade deficit in favor of the foreigner. Is it mere coincidence that America has

31

fallen from being the greatest creditor in the world to the greatest debtor in the world? Even today, when a nation experiences a severe drought, a continuous slump in the economy, or a national trade deficit, it needs to begin examining itself spiritually, to see if it might be out of God's will.

When Elijah prophesied that there would be a famine, he was simply revealing that God was about to do what he had already promised that he would do. God was bringing a famine on Israel to motivate them to repent from their Baal worship. Baal was believed to be the god of the rain, so, when Israel embraced Baal worship, Jehovah God said, "I will cut off all your rain—to show you who is the one true God."

The Prophet Protected

> Then the word of the Lord came to Elijah: "Leave here, turn eastward and hide in the Kerith Ravine, east of the Jordan. You will drink from the brook, and I have ordered the ravens to feed you there" (1 Kings 17:2-4).

When the weather gets bad, some people want to blame the weather forecaster. Ahab and Jezebel were like those who would rather have the doctor touch up the X-rays than admit they need an operation. Instead of admitting the truth and repenting of their sin, they blamed their calamity on Elijah, the weather man. God knew Elijah's life was in danger, so he instructed him to go into hiding in the Kerith Ravine.

Jezebel was about to begin a systematic campaign to kill off all the prophets of the Lord (cf. 1 Kings 18:4). God foresaw her ruthless actions, so he ushered Elijah out of her reach. God will always find a way to protect his people when he has a future mission for them to fulfill. But why, one might ask, did God protect Elijah and allow some of the other prophets to be killed?

In the New Testament, shortly after James was beheaded for preaching the gospel, Peter was imprisoned (Acts 12). Peter's enemies planned to kill him the next day. That night an angel came, opened the gates, and escorted Peter out of prison. Why was Peter protected and James beheaded?

There are no simple answers to those questions. The Christian is compelled to put his faith in the sovereignty of a loving and wise Heavenly Father. When faced with difficult situations, one cannot always say, "God is going to save me," because God does not choose to save everyone from his troubles.

But God knows what he is doing, and the believer can always say with Paul, "For to me, to live is Christ and to die is gain" (Philippians 1:21).

According to respected historian David Barton,[3] an 1856 Maryland textbook carried a fascinating story about George Washington. During the French and Indian War, when George Washington was only twenty-three years old, Great Britain and France were arguing over who owned the colonies. The British sent 2,300 special troops to America. Washington and 1,300 colonial soldiers joined General Braddock to establish supremacy over the French, who had allied with some Indians.

Near what is now Pittsburgh, Pennsylvania, Washington and General Braddock were ambushed by the French-Indian army. As veterans of European wars, the British entered the open field, lined up and fired at their enemy. They were sitting ducks for the Indians and French, who were hiding behind rocks and trees. The lopsided battle continued for two hours, but the British and the colonists were massacred. The British and Americans lost 714 men, compared to 30 French and Indians. George Washington was the only officer left on horseback during the retreat.

The date of the battle was July 17, 1755. The next day Washington described the battle in a letter to his mother. He wrote, "I took off my jacket and there were 4 bullet holes in the jacket. I took off my hat and there were bullet fragments in my hair. God protected me and kept me.

Fifteen years later, George Washington returned to the same Pennsylvania woods. An old Indian heard of Washington's return and traveled several miles to meet him. The Indian said to George Washington, "I told my braves to single you out and fire at you. We knew if we could kill the leaders, we would win the battle. But we could not hit you. I fired at you myself seventeen times, and finally gave up. I traveled here to meet the man whom God would not let die."

That story used to be in every American history book, though it is not today. It seems evident that God had a task for Washington to do, and God protected him for that responsibility.

God does not promise to protect all of us in every circumstance, but there are times when he gives special protection to those he has chosen for a significant duty.

[3]David Barton, *America's Godly Heritage* (Aledo, TX: Wallbuilders, 1990), video tape.

God still had much for Elijah to do, so he made sure Elijah was protected. Obadiah later told Elijah, "There is not a nation or kingdom where my master [Ahab] has not sent someone to look for you" (1 Kings 18:10). There had been an All Points Bulletin out for Elijah, but God had sent him into seclusion before the famine so that Ahab and Jezebel could not lay a finger on him.

The Necessities Provided

"So [Elijah] did what the Lord had told him. He went to the Kerith Ravine, east of the Jordan, and stayed there" (1 Kings 17:5).

Don't get the wrong impression. The Kerith Ravine was not exactly the Hyatt Hotel. Elijah did have his needs met, but there are several factors that indicate Elijah was not vacationing at a first-class resort.

First of all, Elijah was in hiding, and it is never fun to be a fugitive. Elijah was also alone with no telephone, mail ,or outside communication of any kind—probably for several months (long enough for the brook to dry up). Third, he was in rugged territory: not on a beautiful mountainside or beside a scenic lake, but in a ravine.

The final indication that Elijah's conditions were not enviable was his austere diet. Elijah was given bread, water, and morsels of meat twice a day. His diet never varied. The water probably became warm, stagnant, and full of algae as the supply dwindled and finally ran out. Elijah was under spartan conditions.

When a nation experiences God's judgment, Christian people often suffer as well. God "sends rain on the righteous and the unrighteous" (Matthew 5:45). A drought or a bad economy affects everyone.

But the most degrading element of Elijah's diet was the catering service. Elijah received his water by natural means from the brook, but his food was supplied miraculously twice a day by a band of ravens. That may not seem too bad unless you know something about ravens. The Old Testament law declared ravens to be unclean birds. In fact, Leviticus 11:13-15 says ravens are birds that the Israelites were "to detest and not eat because they are detestable." Gary Richmond, a Christian author and former zookeeper at the Los Angeles zoo, explains:

> Ravens are scavengers, therefore they and anything they touch is also unclean. They'll eat just about anything, dead and decaying

meat, rodents, insects, and rotten garbage. They are without taste and are absolutely disgusting. If that weren't enough, it was a well-known fact that ravens store their food in cow dung in order to prevent it from freezing in the winter. They also sift through the cow dung searching for tasty dung beetles.

I'm absolutely sure that Elijah's stomach turned when the first delivery raven arrived. Knowing their habits, he would have wondered where that raven's beak had been just prior to its visit with the food. He may also have known that ravens have an interesting relationship with wolves. Some people believe that ravens have a way of communicating the whereabouts of live food to wolves. Then the ravens get to eat the wolves' leftovers, which generally is a favorite food of theirs anyway.[4]

On a recent mission trip to Africa, my wife and I visited the Massai tribe in a very remote section of Kenya. The people there live in huts made of sticks and manure. The baby goats, sheep, and calves live in the huts with the family. The Massai seldom bathe. The conditions are so unsanitary that the infant mortality rate is about 50%!

The most difficult challenge I had in Kenya was to enter a Massai hut and drink Shai with them. Shai is a tea mixed with milk and sugar and boiled on an open charcoal fire. It is kind of a drink of welcome (like the Indian peace pipe), so I felt compelled to drink it. Although I didn't particularly like the taste, what bothered me the most was drinking out of an old, beaten up tin cup that I was sure had not been washed—just rinsed out in cold water outside the hut. I tend to be a little persnickety when it comes to eating food that may be unclean or drinking water that might be contaminated. I wonder what might really be in my food. Is it properly cooked? Who has been handling this? How is it made? My stomach is weak when it comes to strange foods.

Elijah was in the Kerith Ravine for months, and had to eat food that was highly questionable. His stay at Kerith was no vacation in the tropics. God provided Elijah's every need, but not his every desire. Elijah was being trained in God's university, receiving a major in humility and a minor in sovereignty, and taking a few classes in loneliness, poverty, and faith along the way.

[4]Gary Richmond, *All God's Creatures: Spiritual Lessons from the Animals of the Bible* (Dallas: Word, Inc., 1991), page 164. Used by permission.

The Lord Honored

God's supremacy is confirmed at the end of the story. The brook dried up, and Elijah was sent to sponge from a poverty-stricken widow at Zarephath. But finally, after three and one-half years of famine, God sent Elijah back to confront King Ahab.

"When [Ahab] saw Elijah, he said to him, 'Is that you, you troubler of Israel?'" (1 Kings 18:17). After all this time, Ahab is still blaming Elijah for the famine. But one has to feel a little pity for Ahab. He has been trying to promote the worship of Baal, the god of rain, and it hasn't rained for three and a half years. Ahab's approval rating in the polls has been way down!

> "I have not made trouble for Israel," Elijah replied. "But you and your father's family have. You have abandoned the Lord's commands and have followed the Baals. Now summon the people from all over Israel to meet me on Mount Carmel" (1 Kings 18:18, 19).

On Mount Carmel, Elijah challenged the prophets of Baal to a contest to determine the true God. He said, "Let's have both sides make an altar. I'll call on my God and you call on your god, and the God who consumes his altar with fire will be the true God of Israel."

The prophets of Baal pleaded for a supernatural revelation, there was silence.

When it was Elijah's turn, he ordered twelve large jars of water to be poured on the sacrifice. After three and a half years of famine, he poured water, their most precious commodity, onto the sacrifice! He wanted to demonstrate his trust in the promise and power of his God. When Elijah prayed to Jehovah, a ball of fire came down from heaven, consuming the sacrifice, the wood, the stones and the soil, and licking up the water in the trench (1 Kings 18:38).

"When all the people saw this, they fell prostrate and cried, 'The Lord—he is God! The Lord—he is God!'" (1 Kings 18:39).

At the end of that confrontation, it is recorded: "Meanwhile, the sky grew black with clouds, the wind rose, [and] a heavy rain came on" (1 Kings 18:45).

Elijah's victory on Mount Carmel, and the rain that refreshed the nation, were made possible because a band of ravens kept the prophet alive by catering to him in the Kerith Ravine. Several lessons about obedience can be learned from observing the behavior of the ravens in the Kerith Ravine.

Obedience May Run Counter to One's Instincts

First, the ravens shared, even though it was counter to their instincts. Ravens are scavengers who must fight for their food. The animal kingdom is a violent kingdom, and scavengers battle even their own kind for every morsel. For a raven to have in its possession a piece of meat or bread, and then let go of it, is contrary to its basic nature. But the ravens did so because God commanded it.

To be obedient to Christ one must sometimes go counter to his own instincts.

After Jesus had been fasting for forty days, Satan came to him and said, "Tell these stones to become bread." Satan wanted Jesus to respond to his intense hunger and satisfy himself.

But Jesus denied himself and said, "It is written, 'Man does not live on bread alone, but on every word that comes from the mouth of God'" (Matthew 4:4). Jesus said there would be times when his followers would have to deny themselves, take up their crosses, and follow him.

Some time ago, I was traveling on a local expressway that was under construction. The lanes were narrowed by a solid concrete barrier, and there was no shoulder. I came over the brow of a hill and saw a car not only stopped, but backing up in my lane! The woman driving the car had missed her exit ramp and was attempting to back up about fifty yards on the expressway so she could get off. I could not change lanes because there were cars beside me, so I screeched to a halt about ten yards behind her. I glanced in the rear-view mirror to see whether I was about to get rear-ended. Cars were whipping around me into the fast lane, and I feared someone would come over the brow of the hill, not be able to switch lanes, and plow into the back of my car. I blew my horn, and she turned around and motioned for me to back up! This was a busy expressway under construction, and I was not about to start backing up. I motioned frantically for her to go on. She motioned angrily for me to back up! It was unbelievable! I feverishly shook my head and motioned for her to go on! She finally spotted a break and pulled off into the grass, heading down through a field to get to her exit.

Something like that will destroy your sanctification! Instinctively, I wanted to do what I've seen others do in that situation, but the Bible says we are to be kind to our enemies and pray for those who mistreat us. I prayed, "Lord, protect that woman. Help her to come to know you. Help her to come to our church and let me baptize her, so I can hold her under a long time!"

As Christians, we must at times behave in a way that is counter to our instincts. We want to retaliate, but God's Word commands us to be kind. We instinctively want to horde our possessions, but God tells us to be generous. We are tempted to selfishly gratify our sexual desires, and the world says, "If it feels good, do it!" But God has commanded us to flee fornication.

> So I say, live by the Spirit, and you will not gratify the desires of the sinful nature. For the sinful nature desires what is contrary to the Spirit, and the Spirit what is contrary to the sinful nature. They are in conflict with each other, so that you do not do what you want.... [But] those who belong to Christ Jesus have crucified the sinful nature with its passions and desires (Galatians 5:16, 17, 24).

Obedience Is Right Even When It Is Tedious

The ravens continued to share with Elijah, though the task was tedious. The ravens repeated the process of feeding Elijah twice a day for months. If ravens are anything like humans, they probably perceived the job as an adventure at first and were standing in line to volunteer. But I'm sure the glamour wore off quickly, and the assignment became monotonous. Can't you hear them bickering among themselves? "I did it last week! Why do I always have to go? I'm tired of the hassle. When will I have some time just for me?"

Sometimes a person is reluctant to share himself with others, because he knows that once he begins, he will be expected to continue giving. There are not many one-time gifts in this world.

When Judy and I were first married, I had a bad habit of leaving my clothes on the floor. Judy would graciously pick up after me without complaining, so I didn't think much of it. But eventually I felt guilty and began putting away my own clothes. At first she would be complimentary and appreciative, but now she expects it! It has been years since she said, "Thank you so much for picking up your clothes." Now if I leave them lying around, she'll say, "Hey—forgot something, didn't you?" Isn't it amazing that once you begin giving, people come to expect it as routine?

There are plenty of other, more realistic examples: the Bible college calls you thanking you for your donation, and asks you to please give again; you volunteer to work in the nursery on an emergency basis, and suddenly you are working every Sunday; you agreed to collect for the March of Dimes last summer, and guess who they will depend upon again this year. I sometimes think when you volunteer for something that your name is put on a "soft-heart" list and is passed from one volunteer organization to another!

But God's servant obeys, even if it is not glamorous, even if it means giving repeatedly, and even when it is expected. First Corinthians 16:2 reads, "On the first day of *every* week, each one of you should set aside a sum of money in keeping with his income" (emphasis mine). Sometimes people will try to brag to me about a one-time offering they gave to the church several years back. Those "one-time shots" are nice, but the ones who keep the church going are those who consistently give of their time, money, and talents as part of a daily routine.

Obedience May Go Without Recognition

Finally, the ravens shared, even though there was no recognition. We don't know the names of the ravens who shared with Elijah. No monuments have been built in their honor. Ravens simply don't get much attention, even when they have fulfilled a special assignment for God. We might praise the majesty of an eagle or the grace of a swan, but nobody praises ravens. They are seen as unclean, scavengers, and nuisances. Who wants to pay them any attention?

God does. Jesus said, "Consider the ravens: They do not sow or reap, they have no storeroom or barn; yet God feeds them. And how much more valuable you are than birds!" (Luke 12:24).

God provides for the ravens and cares for them, but on the eternal scale of values, they are not nearly as esteemed as a human being. However, just as the ravens were willing to share without recognition, we should be willing, too.

Be careful not to do your "acts of righteousness" before men, to be seen by them. If you do, you will have no reward from your Father in heaven.

So when you give to the needy, do not announce it with trumpets, as the hypocrites do in the synagogues and on the streets, to be honored by men. I tell you the truth, they have received their reward in full. But when you give to the needy, do not let your left hand know what your right hand is doing, so that your giving may be in secret. Then your Father, who sees what is done in secret, will reward you (Matthew 6:1-4).

Do not give to gain a good reputation or to get your name on a plaque. Give because you have been commanded to be generous, and because God has given to you. Give out of genuine compassion for other people.

I have had the rare privilege of serving at the same church for over twenty-six years. Over the years, the people I have come to appreciate the most are not the up-front people, but those who are consistently behind the scenes, giving on a regular basis without any recognition. Harold Hoover and the Friendship Class have come every Monday morning for four years to clean our 2,500-seat auditorium, though no one ever notices. Every Sunday about forty-five minutes after our last service, Tim and Robin Caine and Dave and Barbara Gillenwater can be seen changing the stage backdrops for our Wednesday night service. People volunteer in our nursery and other areas of the church every week, though they rarely get a "thank you."

Perhaps I appreciate those people because my parents were like that. I never heard my mother sing a solo, and I never heard my father deliver a sermon. But if communion cups needed to be filled, someone needed to cosign on a loan, or a visitor needed a place to stay, they were there. Not many noticed, and they rarely received a thank-you. But God notices.

Jesus said, "I tell you the truth, anyone who gives you a cup of water in my name because you belong to Christ will certainly not lose his reward" (Mark 9:41).

The world calls people foolish who would always give unselfishly, not caring about recognition. But as the martyred missionary Jim Elliot said, "He is no fool who gives up what he cannot keep to gain what he cannot lose."

CHAPTER 3

Do You See What I See?

Numbers 22

A little boy went to his grandfather and asked him to imitate a frog. "Who gave you the idea I could mimic a frog?" Grandpa asked.

"Mom said you could," the boy responded. "I heard her tell Dad that we'll all be rich when you croak!"

If Noah had not saved the animals from the flood, our vocabulary would be much different today. Think of the expressions we use every day that would be meaningless: croak like a frog, quiet as a mouse, slow as a turtle, mean as a junkyard dog, "floats like a butterfly and stings like a bee."

We find phrases inspired by animals even in Scripture. The Bible commands us to be "as shrewd as snakes and as innocent as doves" (Matthew 10:16). Jesus called Herod a "fox" (Luke 13:32), and Peter compared the devil to a roaring lion (1 Peter 5:8).

While animals may enhance our vocabulary, they rarely have vocabularies of their own. But in one of the strangest stories in the Bible, found in Numbers 22, an animal does speak. On that occasion, God used a donkey to speak to a wayward prophet named Balaam. The lessons God taught through a donkey apply not only to Balaam, but to Christians today as well.

The Request of Balaam (Numbers 22:1-7)

The request of Balaam came from Balak, king of Moab. The Israelites were about to launch their attack on the land of Canaan, but Balak was afraid that Israel would attack his country also. He had seen how the Hebrews had destroyed the Amorites. Now those two million Hebrews, searching for a homeland, were pouring into his territory. The Scripture says that all Moab was "filled with dread because of the Israelites" (Numbers 22:3). Balak did not know how to get them out of the region, so he sent for Balaam, the local seer.

> The Moabites said to the elders of Midian, "This horde is going to lick up everything around us, as an ox licks up the grass of the field."
> So Balak son of Zippor, who was king of Moab at that time, sent messengers to summon Balaam son of Beor, who was at Pethor, near the River, in his native land (Numbers 22:4, 5).

This man Balaam is a difficult man to figure out. The Bible usually provides a clear picture of someone's character. The reader almost always knows something about a man's background and his standing with God, but Balaam is the exception. Almost nothing is known about Balaam, which makes him one of the most mysterious and enigmatic characters in the Bible.

Balaam is mentioned more often in the Bible than Mary, the mother of Jesus. The New Testament mentions Balaam three times, and each reference is a warning against apostasy (2 Peter 2:15, Jude 1:11, and Revelation 2:14). But the Bible does not reveal whether Balaam was a prophet of Jehovah or a pagan prophet. Was he God's spokesman or a religious racketeer?

We do know that Balaam was a Midianite who had a wide reputation for being some kind of seer. That prompted Balak to summon Balaam's assistance.

> Balak said: "A people has come out of Egypt; they cover the face of the land and have settled next to me. Now come and put a curse on these people, because they are too powerful for me. Perhaps then I will be able to defeat them and drive them out of the country. For I know that those you bless are blessed, and those you curse are cursed" (Numbers 22:5, 6).

When a military leader faces the unknown, he almost always turns to the supernatural before the battle. In the movie *Patton*, although the general was portrayed as a profane man, there is a scene in which he called for the chaplain before a crucial battle, and the two knelt for prayer. In a similar act, President Bush invited Billy Graham into the White House shortly before the beginning of the Gulf War, and they prayed together.

King Balak wanted the prophet Balaam to come to his home and pronounce a supernatural curse on Israel, whom he was preparing to engage in battle. He sent his elders with a special invitation for Balaam: "The elders of Moab and Midian left, taking with them the fee for divination" (Numbers 22:7).

There are two words in the verse above that give us insight into Balaam's character. The first is *divination*, which means a consultation with the spirits of the underworld, through astrology, palm reading, tea leaves, or other methods. The second word is *fee*, which indicates the men expected Balaam to charge for his services. If Balaam was a prophet of God, it appears he had wandered away from his calling, and was entangled in mysticism and materialism.

The Revelation to Balaam (Numbers 22:8-12)

"'Spend the night here,' Balaam said to them, 'and I will bring you back the answer the Lord gives me'" (Numbers 22:8). What Balaam should have said was, "I can't be bought! Take your money and leave!" Instead, Balaam invited the messengers to wait while he inquired of the Lord, and he would bring back "the Lord's answer."

Balaam was probably a prophet of many gods, claiming to represent any "lord." I think Balaam, like most false prophets, was pretending he would receive a revelation. I would speculate that Balaam was stunned when God actually spoke to him!

An aspiring actor was phoned by his talent agent and told to report to a Broadway theater within the hour. An actor with a small part had become ill and the director needed an immediate replacement. The agent said, "You have only one line: 'Hark, I hear the cannon's roar.' When you step on stage, that's all you have to say."

On the subway ride to the theater, the actor kept rehearsing his line, trying to find the right emphasis. "'*Hark!* I hear the cannon's roar.' No, maybe, 'Hark, I hear the cannon's *roar*.' No, 'Hark, I hear the *cannon's* roar.'"

He arrived at the last moment and quickly changed into his costume, still rehearsing for his moment of glory. He was shoved onto the stage and immediately two explosions boomed off stage. He was so startled that he shouted, "What in the world was that?"

Balaam had been impersonating a prophet, claiming to hear the word of the Lord. When God actually spoke to him, he probably wanted to shout, "Who in the world is that?"

"God came to Balaam and asked, 'Who are these men with you?'" (Numbers 22:9). Balaam explained that they were messengers from Balak, asking him to curse the Israelites. "But God said to Balaam, 'Do not go with them. You must not put a curse on those people, because they are blessed" (Numbers 22:12).

The book of Genesis records God's promise to the patriarch Abraham that he would be the father of a great nation. God had promised Abraham, "I will bless those who bless [your descendants], and whoever curses [them] I will curse" (Genesis 12:3). God warned Balaam not to get involved in a plot to attack the Israelites because they were his chosen people.

The Response of Balaam (Numbers 22:13-22)

Balaam vacillates. He has difficulty making a decision. At first, Balaam gave the correct response. "The next morning Balaam got up and said to Balak's princes, 'Go back to your own country, for the Lord has refused to let me go with you" (Numbers 22:13). God did not want Balaam to put a curse on the Israelites. The answer was, "No," and there was no reason to go. But King Balak did not take "no" for an answer.

Then Balak sent other princes, more numerous and more distinguished than the first. They came to Balaam and said, "This is what Balak son of Zippor says: Do not let anything keep you from coming to me, because I will reward you handsomely and do whatever you say. Come and put a curse on these people for me" (Numbers 22:15-17).

The king sent more impressive representatives, and they fattened the purse. The king thought everyone had a price. He made an offer he was sure Balaam couldn't refuse.

Again, Balaam appeared to give the correct response. "Even if Balak gave me his palace filled with silver and gold, I could not do anything great or small to go beyond the command of the Lord my God" (Numbers 22:18).

Then Balaam said, "Now go home!" and he slammed the door, right? No, that's not what happened.

Balaam said, "Now stay here tonight as the others did, and I will find out what else the Lord will tell me" (Numbers 22:19).

Balaam was beginning to waver. The offer was attractive. He could use the money. He could use the prestige. He thought, "Maybe God will change his mind if I ask again." His greed was getting the better of him.

Balaam was like the preacher who informed his wife he had received an offer from another church that would double his salary. He said, "I'm going down to my study to pray about it. You go upstairs and pack!"

We would do well to remember that the easiest time to resist temptation is at the first request. The easiest time to say "no" to a vacuum salesman is as soon as you answer the door. If you know you don't want his product, but you let him come inside out of courtesy, it becomes more difficult to say "no." The longer he stays and the longer the demonstration continues, the more obligated you feel, and the more difficult it is to say, "I'm sorry, I'm not buying."

The best time to resist temptation is at the first appeal. If it is wrong, say "no" immediately. The longer you flirt with the opportunity, the more difficult it becomes to resist. That is the reason the Bible commands us to "flee sexual immorality" (1 Corinthians 6:18). The old country preacher said, "If you don't intend to go in the house, stay off the front porch."

Balaam did not resist forcefully enough. He said, "You spend the night, and I'll think it over."

God's answer to Balaam is surprising: "That night God came to Balaam and said, 'Since these men have come to summon you, go with them, but do only what I tell you'" (Numbers 22:20).

God didn't want Balaam to go, but he let him go anyway. God sometimes permits us to do what we want to do, even if it is not in his perfect will. He may allow us to do so, but we must accept the consequences. He may permit us to do what is not in our own best interest or His, but we must reap the harvest. Balaam wanted to accept the money, so God permitted him to go with Balak's men. But it was not in God's perfect will, and neither was it in Balaam's best interest.

"Balaam got up in the morning, saddled his donkey and went with the princes of Moab" (Numbers 22:21).

The Resistance to Balaam (Numbers 22:22-33)

The donkey that Balaam was riding proved to be more sensitive to God's leading than the prophet himself. The donkey resisted.

But God was very angry when he went, and the angel of the Lord stood in the road to oppose him. Balaam was riding on his donkey and his two servants were with him. When the donkey saw the angel of the Lord standing in the road with a drawn sword in his hand, she turned off the road into a field. Balaam beat her to get her back on the road (Numbers 22:22, 23).

Some animals have a sixth sense that allows them to detect danger sooner than humans do. Their hearing may be keener, their eyesight sharper, or their sense of smell more acute. Balaam's donkey was given the ability to see an angel that the "seer" couldn't see. The angel's sword was drawn. He was not the angel of peace, but the angel of death. Balaam's donkey wisely turned off the road into a field. But Balaam, mistaking his beast's behavior for rebellion, beat her back onto the road. Then the angel reappeared.

Then the angel of the Lord stood in a narrow path between two vineyards, with walls on both sides. When the donkey saw the angel of the Lord, she pressed close to the wall, crushing Balaam's foot against it. So he beat her again (Numbers 22:24, 25).

I can be sympathetic with Balaam. It is difficult not to lose your temper with a rebellious animal, especially if it hurts you physically. As a boy, I had to milk our cows in the mornings, and there were times when one of our cows, Suzie, would decide she didn't want to be milked. I would have to search deep into the woods to find her. When I finally got her to the barn, she would refuse to walk into her stanchion. When the milking began, she would switch her tail and hit me in the eyes. Then occasionally, about two-thirds of the way through the milking, she would stick her foot in the bucket, ruining all the milk. I am convinced she did it out of spite! That was usually all I could take, and I would smack her across the backside. I doubt that she could feel it, but it did help to ventilate my anger!

I heard of a Quaker who had a rebellious cow like Suzie. After he had endured all he could take, he said to the cow, "Thou knowest that I am a Quaker and a pacifist and cannot strike thee. But what thou dost not know is that tomorrow, I am going to sell thee to a Baptist!"

Balaam was exasperated with his donkey, especially after his foot was crushed, and he beat her. But the donkey resisted Balaam's direction a third time.

Then the angel of the Lord moved on ahead and stood in a narrow place where there was no room to turn, either to the right or to the left. When the donkey saw the angel of the Lord, she lay down under Balaam, and he was angry and beat her with his staff (Numbers 22:26, 27).

This poor donkey is getting brutalized! Balaam cannot understand why she refuses to cooperate. Then the strangest thing happens.

Then the Lord opened the donkey's mouth, and she said to Balaam, "What have I done to you to make you beat me these three times?" (Numbers 22:28).

The donkey speaks to Balaam, and registers a protest! When my son Rusty was about five years old, I read him this story for the first time. When I came to the part about the donkey talking, he said, "Are you kidding me, Dad?" This story does not sound reasonable, even to a child. Did the donkey really talk, or is this simply a myth that developed over the years?

We do not think it strange when toy manufacturers make a talking doll or talking teddy bear. We do not ask questions when television producers use special effects to create a talking horse like Mr. Ed. Is it unreasonable to think that God, the producer of this universe, could speak through a donkey that he had created?

If God could speak to Moses through a burning bush, he could surely choose to speak to an apostate prophet through a donkey. Our God is a God of miracles! Causing a donkey to speak would be no more difficult than walking on water or raising the dead. As Luke 1:37 says, "Nothing is impossible with God."

I think the strangest part of the miracle is that Balaam did not seemed shocked by it! He carried on a dialogue with his donkey as if it were normal.

[The donkey] said to Balaam, "What have I done to you to make you beat me these three times?"

Balaam answered the donkey, "You have made a fool of me! If I had a sword in my hand, I would kill you right now."

The donkey said to Balaam, "Am I not your own donkey, which you have always ridden, to this day? Have I been in the habit of doing this to you?"

"No," he said (Numbers 22:28-30).

This is hilarious! The donkey defends her record. "I've been a good donkey," she says. "Look at my record. Do you think I'd disobey you for no reason at all?"

The Repentance of Balaam (Numbers 22:31-35)

Then the Lord opened Balaam's eyes, and he saw the angel of the Lord standing in the road with his sword drawn. So he bowed low and fell facedown (Numbers 22:31).

Balaam was an internationally known seer, but he had been blind to spiritual reality. His donkey had seen what he was too blind to notice.

The angel of the Lord asked him, "Why have you beaten your donkey these three times? I have come here to oppose you because your path is a reckless one before me. The donkey saw me and turned away from me these three times. If she had not turned away, I would certainly have killed you by now, but I would have spared her" (Numbers 22:32, 33).

The donkey that Balaam had been abusing had spared his life. Balaam should have been grateful.

Balaam said to the angel of the Lord, "I have sinned. I did not realize you were standing in the road to oppose me. Now if you are displeased, I will go back."
The angel of the Lord said to Balaam, "Go with the men, but speak only what I tell you." So Balaam went with the princes of Balak (Numbers 22:34, 35).

When Balaam arrived at the palace, King Balak urged Balaam to place a curse on his enemies, the Israelites. But Balaam had learned his lesson. Four times the king tried to persuade Balaam to change his mind. But even when Balak's anger burned against him (Numbers 24:10), Balaam prophesied only the message of God. He refused to place a curse on God's people.

There are three lessons about spiritual truth to be learned from Balaam's donkey.

The Spiritually Discerning See the Unseen
Balaam's donkey could see the unseen. While Balaam was blind to spiritual reality, the donkey saw the angel. Paul wrote,

"So we fix our eyes not on what is seen, but on what is unseen. For what is seen is temporary, but what is unseen is eternal" (2 Corinthians 4:18).

We live in two distinct worlds: the physical world that we can see and touch and smell, and the spiritual world that we cannot see with our eyes. Angels, demons, God, and Satan can be seen only by those who are spiritually discerning.

We think of the material world as the real world, but Paul insists the opposite is true. When you look at me, you don't really see me. You see the physical body that I live in. My body is only a house for my spirit, which you cannot see. Some day, my body will be put in the grave and will decompose. But that which is unseen, my spirit, is eternal. Paul wrote in 2 Corinthians 5:1, "Now we know that if the earthly tent we live in is destroyed, we have a building from God, an eternal house in heaven, not built by human hands."

It should not be difficult for us to believe in a world that we cannot see. We don't see sound waves, but we know they exist. We don't see X-rays, but we know that too much exposure to them can be harmful. I push a remote control button, and the television channel changes, though I can see no connection. Atoms and molecules, the basic structures of the universe, cannot be seen with the naked eye, but we are confident they exist.

Though I have not seen Jesus, God, or angels with my physical eyes, I believe and know that they exist. Jesus told Thomas, "Because you have seen me, you have believed; blessed are those who have not seen and yet have believed" (John 20:29).

In 2 Kings 6, the king of Aram was angry with the prophet Elisha. He sent a strong military force and surrounded the city where Elisha was living. When Elisha's servant got up the next morning, he saw the army and panicked. But Elisha prayed for his servant, and the servant was given a glimpse into the spirit world:

> When the servant of the man of God got up and went out early the next morning, an army with horses and chariots had surrounded the city. "Oh, my lord, what shall we do?" the servant asked.
>
> "Don't be afraid," the prophet answered. "Those who are with us are more than those who are with them."
>
> And Elisha prayed, "O Lord, open his eyes so he may see." Then the Lord opened the servant's eyes, and he looked and saw the hills full of horses and chariots of fire all around Elisha" (2 Kings 6:15-17).

As we mature in Christ, we should learn to see beyond the physical. Perhaps we cannot see the angels as literally as Elisha's servant could, but we should gain an ability to perceive the spirit world. Jesus said, "For where two or three come together in my name, there am I with them" (Matthew 18:20). Lanny Wolfe wrote the words to a familiar chorus:

> Surely the presence of the Lord is in this place;
> I can feel his mighty power and his grace.
> I can hear the brush of angels' wings,
> I see glory on each face.
> Surely the presence of the Lord is in this place.[5]

Have you ever been through a moving worship service and felt the presence of God? You were uplifted and challenged, there was spiritual food served from the Word of God; perhaps there were tears and laughter. You knew God was there, and you hated to see it end. Then, when the final "Amen" was spoken, the person in front of you turned around and said, "What did you think of Friday night's game?" Did his comment seem out of place for a moment? There is certainly nothing wrong with talking about a ball game, but shouldn't we feel a sense of reverence and appreciation, at least for a few moments, knowing that we have been in the presence of the King, standing on holy ground?

"So we fix our eyes not on what is seen, but on what is unseen. For what is seen is temporary, but what is unseen is eternal" (2 Corinthians 4:18).

The Spiritually Discerning Stand for the Unpopular

Balaam's donkey took a stand for an unpopular position. She refused to give in, even though it wasn't the popular thing to do.

We usually think of stubbornness as a negative trait. But stubbornness is a positive characteristic when it refers to someone who is determined to do what is right. In the Bible, it is called "perseverance," "steadfastness," or "faithfulness."

One Sunday when I was a senior in high school, my friends asked me to go with them to Lake Erie for the afternoon. We had a great time cruising in our convertibles, swimming in the

---

[5]"Surely the Presence," © 1977 by Lanny Wolfe Music/ASCAP. All rights controlled by Pathway Music, Box 2250, Cleveland, TN 37320. Used by permission.

lake, and flirting with the girls on the beach. Late in the afternoon, someone said, "Let's go to my parents' cottage and have a cook out."

I said, "I've got to go home."

"Come on, Russell," everybody said. "You can't leave now. The fun is just starting."

I insisted I had to leave. A good friend took me aside and asked why I couldn't stay. I said, "Well, it's my dad. He thinks on Sunday night I'm supposed to be in church."

He said, "I know your dad—he's a great guy! Just call him up and tell him you're having fun! He'll understand."

I said, "No, you don't know that side of my dad. It's no use. We go, no matter what. He doesn't waver on that."

I didn't call; I didn't beg. I just headed for home. I already knew what the answer would be. (I had dared to ask only a couple of times before.) "As long as you live under my roof and eat meals at my table," I could hear him saying, "you will go to church Sunday mornings, Sunday nights, and Wednesday nights. When you are on your own, you can decide for yourself." By the time I was on my own, I'd been brainwashed!

No, I had simply been trained in how to develop good habits, and how to remain steadfast. Some may have thought my dad was stubborn, unyielding, rigid and uncompromising. I think God was pleased with his perseverance and faithfulness.

Paul wrote, "Let us not become weary in doing good, for at the proper time we will reap a harvest if we do not give up" (Galatians 6:9).

The donkey stood her ground, even though she suffered for it. Three times Balaam beat her! Then he threatened to kill her with a sword. She was the victim of physical and verbal abuse.

When you stand your ground, there will be times when your own children will harass you, society will threaten you, even some Christians may try to beat on you. But the Lord honors those who stand their ground under persecution.

Jesus said:

Blessed are those who are persecuted because of righteousness, for theirs is the kingdom of heaven. Blessed are you when people insult you, persecute you and falsely say all kinds of evil against you because of me. Rejoice and be glad, because great is your reward in heaven, for in the same way they persecuted the prophets who were before you (Matthew 5:10-12).

Some time ago in one of my sermons, I was critical of our local board of aldermen for proposing an ordinance that would endorse homosexuality. I received a number of reinforcing and appreciative letters, but there were some negative reactions, too. One woman wrote that she and her husband had been attending our church for seven months but would not be returning because of an "unenlightened and unsympathetic stand" from the pulpit.

> Therefore, my dear brothers, stand firm. Let nothing move you. Always give yourselves fully to the work of the Lord, because you know that your labor in the Lord is not in vain (1 Corinthians 15:58).

> Watch your life and doctrine closely. Persevere in them, because if you do, you will save both yourself and your hearers (1 Timothy 4:16).

> See that what you have heard from the beginning remains in you. If it does, you also will remain in the Son and in the Father. And this is what he has promised us—even eternal life (1 John 2:24, 25).

God calls us to be as stubborn as Balaam's donkey in standing for what is right, even though it may be unpopular.

The Spiritually Discerning Speak the Unexpected

Finally, Balaam's donkey spoke the unexpected. The donkey was a dumb animal, and she was expected to keep her mouth shut. She was inferior to Balaam. Perhaps she felt unworthy. But God used her to speak a powerful message to a wayward prophet.

Sometimes after I preach a sermon, someone will come to me and say, "God really spoke through you this morning." It is a nice compliment, but I am not tempted to feel proud after a compliment like that. I always remember that God once spoke through a donkey! If he speaks through me, I have no reason to become prideful.

Though Balaam may not have expected it, Balaam's donkey spoke exactly what God wanted her to say. It wasn't earth-shattering. She didn't predict the outcome of the war, or reveal the secrets of Balaam's past. She didn't give him the theory of relativity years in advance. She asked three simple questions: (1) What have I done to merit this beating? (2) Haven't I been faithful to you? (3) Have I been in the habit of doing this to you?

God does not usually give us spectacular speeches to recite when we are being persecuted. He wants us to state the simple truth. The truth has power in itself. People do not have to be impressed with our intellect or creativity. They just need to be asked simple questions: Where did you come from? Where are you going? Why are you here? What do you think about Jesus? What is your source of truth?

Several years ago, Dr. James Kennedy of Coral Ridge Presbyterian Church in Fort Lauderdale, Florida, began an "evangelism explosion" by training his people to ask two simple questions: "If you were to die tonight, are you confident you would go to Heaven?" and "If you stood at the gate of Heaven, why should God let you in?" Those simple questions opened many doors and alerted thousands to their need for Jesus Christ.

We often excuse ourselves from speaking out for God because we think we are not qualified. We feel we should know more about the Bible, and we feel inferior to the intellectuals around us. We timidly say, "I'll just let my light shine and hope people will see Jesus living in me."

The donkey was no match intellectually for Balaam, but she refused to be intimidated. She stubbornly spoke the truth as God revealed it. The Scriptures remind us to speak the truth in love. We have a responsibility simply to be ambassadors. We are to speak the truth that the Lord has already given us in his Word. We must deliver it as clearly and lovingly as possible, but we cannot remain silent. God has promised that when we speak out in faith, he will take care of the rest: "My word that goes out from My mouth: it will not return to me empty, but will accomplish what I desire and achieve the purpose for which I sent it" (Isaiah 55:11).

Bob Moorehead, the minister of Overlake Christian Church in Seattle, tells of a new, enthusiastic Christian named Mark, who was not a very impressive witness. Mark had only a third-grade education and was not very polished. But he insisted on enrolling in the evangelism training class, hoping to become a regular caller.

Bob admits he hoped Mark wouldn't pass, but he did. On about Mark's third night of calling, the secretary made a mistake. Mark was sent to call on an attorney and his wife who had been attending the church. Mark's prep card read, "Bill and Jean have been called on twice, but continue to reject Jesus Christ."

Bob learned later what happened in that call. Mark entered their home, skipped the polite small talk and went straight to the point. He said, "This card says you continue to reject Jesus Christ. I want to know if you are going to reject Jesus again tonight, because if you do, you are going to Hell."

The husband cleared his throat, glanced at his wife and said, "Well, we've never had anyone put it quite that bluntly before."

Mark said, "You do believe in Jesus, don't you?"

The man said, "Yes, but. . . ."

"Don't say, 'But,'" Mark said, "People go to Hell that way. Is there any reason why you and your wife cannot kneel with me right now and accept Jesus Christ?"

The man looked at his wife, and said, "Well, Jean, what do you think?"

She said, "I think it's time."

They knelt and prayed. Mark later took them to the church building and saw to it that they were baptized. He walked into the secretary's office and said, "Who's next?"

It is easy to worry so much about saying the right thing, having the right timing, and showing tact that one ends up saying nothing at all. Technique is not nearly as important as conviction. If God spoke through a donkey, he can speak through us, if we will see what is unseen, stand for what is sometimes unpopular, and speak, even when it is unexpected.

CHAPTER 4

Facing the Lions

Daniel 6

There is an old story about a college student who was desperately in need of a summer job. He searched the want ads and discovered the local zoo was looking for help. He couldn't think of a more creative way to spend the summer, but he wasn't prepared for the job description. When he went to apply, the zookeeper explained that they had recently lost their gorilla. "You can't have a zoo without a gorilla," the zookeeper rationalized. "We are expecting a new gorilla by the end of the summer, but, in the meantime, we need someone to dress the part. We'll pay you well."

The young student was hesitant, but he needed the money, so he agreed. After a couple of hours in the gorilla suit, he found himself almost enjoying the job. But in the awkward costume he could not always see where he was going, and he accidently stumbled into the lion's cage. The lion roared violently, throwing the college student into a panic. "Help!" he screamed. "Help! I'm a man in here! I'm a man in this gorilla suit!"

Then he heard a voice from inside the lion whisper, "Shut up, kid! You'll get us both fired!"

In reality, it would be impossible for a human to imitate the roar of the king of the jungle. I read recently that a lion's roar can be heard up to five miles away! If you have ever stood near a lion when he roars, you know that the sound, as if it were coming from a giant bass speaker, will vibrate through your whole body. It is a powerful roar that is used by the lion to strike a paralyzing fear into his prey.[6]

---

[6]Gary Richmond, *All God's Creatures*, p. 8.

The prey of the lion has reason to be afraid. A hungry lion can eat thirty percent of his body weight in one sitting. That's like an average man eating 200 quarter-pound hamburgers for lunch! If the lion is hungry enough, he is not beyond attacking a human being, and he possesses the strength of fourteen men![7]

The Old Testament story of Daniel and the lions' den is very familiar to most Christians, but it takes on added significance when one considers the immense power of a lion. Daniel could have been expected to react with terror when he was thrown into that den, but he faced the beasts with courage. Let's look back at that old story with renewed appreciation for the courage of Daniel.

The Story

Daniel was a Jewish man who was taken from his homeland at a young age and forced to live in the pagan land of Babylon. He was a foreigner—a Hebrew living in a Gentile country. He would have talked differently, behaved differently, perhaps even dressed differently, and he practiced a different religion from the pagan religion of those around him. Yet Daniel withstood the peer pressure and remained faithful to his God. The Lord rewarded him by granting him political success.

> It pleased Darius to appoint 120 satraps to rule throughout the kingdom, with three administrators over them, one of whom was Daniel. The satraps were made accountable to them so that the king might not suffer loss (Daniel 6:1, 2).

The Babylonian kingdom had recently been conquered by the new world ruler, Darius the Mede. Daniel had been a high-ranking ruler in Babylon under the reign of Belshazzar. One might have expected the conqurering king to execute all the top officials of the old regime, but King Darius liked Daniel and decided to make him one of his three top advisers. Daniel was so successful that he was about to become the second most powerful man in the world.

> Now Daniel so distinguished himself among the administrators and the satraps by his exceptional qualities that the king planned to set him over the whole kingdom (Daniel 6:3).

---

[7]Gary Richmond, *All God's Creatures*, pp. 11, 30.

The other politicians couldn't handle Daniel's success. They began plans for a smear campaign.

> At this, the administrators and the satraps tried to find grounds for charges against Daniel in his conduct of government affairs, but they were unable to do so. They could find no corruption in him, because he was trustworthy and neither corrupt nor negligent (Daniel 6:4).

Daniel's competitors probably stopped at nothing. I imagine they interviewed his female co-workers, followed him home from work and eavesdropped on his conversations. If it had been possible, they would have bugged his telephone, scrutinized his tax records, and examined his bank statements. Yet they found nothing. He was "trustworthy and neither corrupt nor negligent." Not only was he honest, he was a hard worker. There was nothing in his past, nothing about his personal life, and nothing about his work ethic that was the least bit newsworthy.

A small-town prosecuting attorney said to an elderly woman on the witness stand, "Ma'am, do you know who I am?"

"Yes," she said, "I do. I've watched you grow up. I know that you are a liar and a thief, and you have cheated your way to the top."

"Do you know the defense attorney?" he asked, hoping to redeem himself.

"Yes, I do," she replied. "I've watched him grow up, too. I know that he is also a liar and a thief, and he has cheated his way to the top."

The judge demanded a recess and called both attorneys to his chambers. The judge said to the prosecuting attorney, "Son, I don't know where you got that lady, but I'll throw you in jail for contempt of court if you ask her if she knows me!"

It is unfortunate that we nearly expect a politician to be corrupt, but it is refreshing to read that Daniel's enemies could find nothing wrong with him. I wonder how many of today's politicians could have passed that test. I wonder how many of us could have passed it, for that matter. How desperately we need more godly people like Daniel in the political arena!

"Finally these men said, 'We will never find any basis for charges against this man Daniel unless it has something to do with the law of his God'" (Daniel 6:5). Daniel's only idiosyncrasies emerged from his religious practices. His enemies knew they would only find something wrong with Daniel if they could find something wrong with his religion. That gave someone a cunning idea.

Daniel's competitors went to King Darius and convinced him to pass a statute outlawing prayer.

> So the administrators and the satraps went as a group to the king and said: "O King Darius, live forever! The royal administrators, prefects, satraps, advisers and governors have all agreed that the king should issue an edict and enforce the decree that anyone who prays to any god or man during the next thirty days, except to you, O king, shall be thrown into the lions' den" (Daniel 6:6, 7).

It is difficult to know how they could have convinced King Darius to do such an egotistical thing. They must have said, "O Great Darius, you are the king, the great savior of this nation! We want to be insured that you have the undivided devotion of the people of your land. We have discovered that some people are tempted to 'pray' to other gods, O king! Only you should receive that kind of honor. Anything else would be disloyal."

They convinced King Darius to put the decree in writing, which meant, according to the Laws of the Medes and Persians, that even the king himself could not repeal the law. They had stroked the king's ego, and he bit the bait.

It seemed Daniel was in a quandary. Would he compromise his faith to maintain his political viability? Would he suspend his practice of praying three times a day until the month had passed? Would he continue to pray, but do it in secret? Not Daniel! Upon discovering that prayer had become a capital crime, he did the same thing he had been doing every day. Even though he knew his enemies would be policing his every move, he boldly continued his practice of praying.

> Now when Daniel learned that the decree had been published, he went home to his upstairs room where the windows opened toward Jerusalem. Three times a day he got down on his knees and prayed, giving thanks to his God, just as he had done before (Daniel 6:10).

What happened next is familiar to almost everyone. Daniel was dragged before the king, and with much regret King Darius sent Daniel to the den of lions.

Daniel should have been trembling with fright. There may have been as many as forty lions in the pit where Daniel was thrown. When a lions' den was used for capital punishment, the lions would be kept hungry in anticipation of an execution. Daniel did not expect to live—unless God intervened. Yet there is no hint that Daniel was afraid. He faced what seemed to be sure death courageously.

The great missionary David Livingston was once attacked by a lion. He described how the lion grabbed him up in its jaws and shook him, throwing him into a stupor, like the stupor of a mouse that has been shaken by a cat. In the mouth of the lion, Livingston could no longer feel pain or fear, but he was completely conscious of what was happening. Thankfully, the lion was shot and died before it could take the life of the great missionary.[8]

Daniel expected to endure a similar experience when he was thrown into the lions' den, but God miraculously closed the lions' mouths.

> Then the king returned to his palace and spent the night without eating and without any entertainment being brought to him. And he could not sleep.
>
> At the first light of dawn, the king got up and hurried to the lions' den. When he came near the den, he called to Daniel in an anguished voice, "Daniel, servant of the living God, has your God, whom you serve continually, been able to rescue you from the lions?"
>
> Daniel answered, "O king, live forever! My God sent this angel, and he shut the mouths of the lions. They have not hurt me, because I was found innocent in his sight. Nor have I ever done any wrong before you, O king" (Daniel 6:18-22).

King Darius was ecstatic, and immediately repented of the ungodly decree he had established.

> The king was overjoyed and gave orders to lift Daniel out of the den. And when Daniel was lifted from the den, no wound was found on him, because he had trusted in his God.
>
> At the king's command, the men who had falsely accused Daniel were brought in and thrown into the lions' den, along with their

---

[8]Gary Richmond, *All God's Creatures*, pp. 15-19.

wives and children. And before they reached the floor of the den, the lions overpowered them and crushed all their bones (Daniel 6:23, 24).

It is possible that all 122 of the administrators and satraps were thrown into the lions' den, along with their wives and children! And they were mauled before they reached the ground! That shows the awesome power of hungry lions, but more importantly, it proves the miraculous power of the Almighty God, who shut the mouths of those same lions to protect his servant Daniel.

King Darius then issued a new decree, commanding that all people fear and reverence Daniel's God.

> For he is the living God and he endures forever. . . . He rescues and he saves; he performs signs and wonders in the heavens and on the earth. He has rescued Daniel from the power of the lions (Daniel 6:26, 27).

Most of us do not have to face a literal lion as Daniel and David Livingston did, but the Bible makes it clear that we have an even more formidable foe: "Be self-controlled and alert. Your enemy the devil prowls around like a roaring lion looking for someone to devour" (1 Peter 5:8). Peter compared the workings of Satan to the prowling of a hungry lion. There are several similarities between the dangers Satan poses and the dangers of a roaring lion.

Satan's Greatest Asset is Fear

Just as a lion's roar strikes fear into its victims, Satan will try to paralyze you with fear; so be courageous.

If a person were asked to walk across an eight-inch wide board that was only six inches above the ground, he would probably have no problem. But if that board were fifty feet above the ground, his chances of falling would be much greater. The only difference is fear.

Satan will do his best to change people's perspective. He will roar loudly to strike terror into their heart. He wants them to experience the fear of failure, so he roars, "What if you're not good enough?"

He wants them to feel the fear of rejection, so he roars, "What if they don't like you?"

He wants them to be plagued with the fear of doubt, so he

roars, "What if there really is no God? What if he doesn't care?"

Satan wants them to experience the fear of the unknown, so he roars, "What if the future is painful? What if death is lonely? What if there is nothing on the other side?"

When Satan tempts us to be paralyzed by fear, we must remember what has been written in God's Word:

> For God did not give us a spirit of timidity, but a spirit of power, of love and of self discipline (1 Timothy 1:7).

> Surely God is my salvation; I will trust and not be afraid. The Lord, the Lord, is my strength and my song; he has become my salvation (Isaiah 12:2).

Daniel, with great courage, knelt and prayed three times a day, though he was sure it would cost him his life. He did not let fear paralyze him. When we allow fear to motivate our decisions or make us indecisive, unless it is the fear of God, we have become paralyzed by Satan's roar. He and his allies are prowling around like roaring lions, but God's Word says:

> Be strong and courageous. Do not be afraid or terrified because of them, for the Lord your God goes with you; he will never leave you nor forsake you (Deuteronomy 31:6).

Satan is Powerful

It is not enough to simply face Satan with courage. He is powerful; so do not fight him alone. Just as Daniel and David Livingston could never have defeated the lions alone, we cannot defeat Satan without the power of God.

In the book of Judges, Samson overcame a lion and hundreds of Philistines with only the power of God. But Samson allowed his hair—the symbol of his devotion to God—to be cut. Trusting in his own strength, he failed to rely on God, who was the true source of his supernatural power. He became as weak as any other man, and he was overtaken by the Philistines.

If we try to fight Satan on our own strength, we are sure to be defeated. But there is good news. There is another who is compared to a lion in the Bible—Jesus Christ, the "Lion of Judah." And the Bible makes it clear that the Lion of Judah is much more powerful than Satan.

In fact, Scriptures like Hebrews 2:14 make it clear that the devil has already been defeated. When Christ died on the cross, then rose from the dead, he won the battle over Satan's most powerful weapon. Christ emerged victorious, Satan was defeated, and we have nothing to fear if we will rely on Christ's power instead of our own.

> Since the children have flesh and blood, he too shared in their humanity so that by his death he might destroy him who holds the power of death—that is, the devil—and free those who all their lives were held in slavery by their fear of death (Hebrews 2:14, 15).

> God anointed Jesus of Nazareth with the Holy Spirit and power, and . . . he went around doing good and healing all who were under the power of the devil, because God was with him (Acts 10:38).

Charles Stanley tells of a time when he was struggling with a lot of opposition. In the midst of the turmoil, an elderly member of his church invited him to her apartment for lunch. He hesitated because he was busy and did not want to listen to her lecture, but he finally agreed.

He met her downstairs at the retirement community where she lived. They had lunch together, and then she explained there was something she wanted to show him in her apartment. She took him to a picture hanging on her living room wall, a picture of Daniel in the lions' den. "Son," she said, "look at this picture and tell me what you see."

Stanley looked at the picture and saw that all the lions had their mouths closed. Some were lying down and some were standing. Daniel was standing with his hands behind him looking up at the ray of light coming into the den. Stanley pointed out every detail he could think of. "Is there anything else?" she asked.

He could think of nothing. She put her arm on his shoulder and said, "Son, what I want you to see is that Daniel doesn't have his eyes on the lions, but on Christ."

> Let us fix our eyes on Jesus, the author and perfecter of our faith, who for the joy set before him endured the cross, scorning its shame, and sat down at the right hand of the throne of God (Hebrews 12:2).

CHAPTER 5

The God of
Second Chances

Jonah 1–4

There is an old saying that, when a dog bites a man, it's not news; but when a man bites a dog, that makes headlines. When a man catches a fish, that's normal; it's no big deal. But when a fish catches a man, that gets our attention! The story of Jonah, who was caught, swallowed, saved, and delivered by a special fish is one of the most colorful stories in the Bible.

This, of course, is a story that is often ridiculed by the skeptics. They scoff at the idea that a man could live for three days and three nights in the belly of a fish and then be coughed up on shore and come out preaching. To the unbeliever, this story ranks right up there with the fairy tale of the cow that jumped over the moon! Even some who believe most of the Bible just can't accept this story of Jonah as a historical account. To some sophisticated minds, it seems too fantastical, so they explain it away as a parable. They will say this story really wasn't meant to be taken literally: God was just trying to teach a lesson about obedience.

But I accept the story of Jonah as an actual account, and I do so for two reasons. The first is the reliability of the Scriptures. The Bible is reliable in every facet. Second Timothy 3:16 says, "All Scripture is given by inspiration of God" (KJV). Bible-believing Christians, who believe other accounts of Scripture as being factual—the parting of the Red Sea, the calling down of fire from Heaven, the raising of Lazarus from the dead—should have no problem accepting this account. If one accepts other supernatural events as literal, there is no reason to dismiss this story as fictional.

It seems to me that if one believes the first verse of the Bible, he won't have any trouble with the rest. "In the beginning, God created the heavens and the earth." God is so powerful that he could create this vast universe. As the angel said to Mary, "Nothing is impossible with God."

The second reason I believe this story is that Jesus believed it. Jesus said, "As Jonah was three days and three nights in the belly of a huge fish, so the Son of Man will be three days and three nights in the heart of the earth" (Matthew 12:40). Now some people will say that Jesus was just accommodating the limited mindset of his day. But Jesus said, "I am truth. . . . My word is truth." He referred to this story as being a literal event. He used it to picture his resurrection, which was an actual resurrection.

Rather than get bogged down in the arguments about the literal nature of the story, however, the reader is encouraged simply to accept it as fact. Having done so, it is then possible to examine it for its meaning and to learn some of the lessons that Jonah learned from the fish that went manning.

The Defiance of Jonah

> The Word of the Lord came to Jonah son of Amittai: "Go to the great city of Nineveh and preach against it, because its wickedness has come up before me" (Jonah 1:1, 2).

I guarantee you that no preacher would have wanted this assignment. Nineveh was a very wicked city. As a matter of fact, the Living Bible paraphrases it, "Its wickedness smells to high heaven." Nineveh was noted for its prostitution, its witchcraft, its cruelty in war; they were known to have skinned their enemies alive. Jonah didn't want to go. And it was an enemy city. Some have even speculated that the Ninevites may have killed Jonah's parents. And that would have made him bitter. It was a distant city—Nineveh was 500 miles away from Jonah's home of Gathheifer. That was a long way to travel on foot. So it's easy to understand why Jonah didn't find this assignment very appealing. He defied God's order and went in the opposite direction.

> But Jonah ran away from the Lord and headed for Tarshish. He went down to Joppa, where he found a ship bound for that port. After paying the fare, he went aboard and sailed for Tarshish to flee from the Lord (Jonah 1:3).

When my wife and I were making plans to go to Kenya, somebody gave me a clipping from the Louisville *Courier-Journal*. The heading read: "Violence against foreigners threatens tourism in cash hungry Kenya." The article reported on a series of incidents in a popular wildlife reserve, the Masai Mara, an area about a hundred twenty-five miles southwest of Nairobi. Men had been attacked, one guide had been killed, the women had been raped. When it came time to go to Kenya, I wanted to go to Hawaii instead—the Hawaiians need the Lord, too!

Jonah didn't want to go to Nineveh. It was a wicked and dangerous city. So he rebelled and headed for Tarshish. He could preach there.

Everything seemed to go well at first for Jonah. He arrived safely in Joppa, there was a ship headed for Tarshish that had a vacancy, there was a ticket available, he had the resources, and he bought the ticket. Everything was going smoothly. But we always have to be careful not to interpret favorable circumstances as God's approval.

Favorable circumstances can be a coincidence or they can be the work of the devil. I have talked with men who have run off with somebody else's wife, and they say, "Well, I really didn't plan it that way. It just happened naturally. I mean, we had so much in common, we enjoyed each other's company, and it reminded us of how miserable we had been. We just concluded that this must be God's will for our lives because He knew how unhappy we both were in our previous circumstance—and now we are so happy!" We succumb to a dangerous ploy of Satan when we determine "God's will" by circumstances or by feelings instead of commandments. Jonah was so comfortable at first in his defiance that he went down into the hold of the ship and went to sleep. But it was the calm before the storm. God was very displeased.

The Discipline From God

> Then the Lord sent a great wind on the sea, and such a violent storm arose that the ship threatened to break up. All the sailors were afraid and each cried out to his own god. And they threw the cargo into the sea to lighten the ship (Jonah 1:4, 5).

It must be a bad storm when sailors are afraid. When sailors pray, it's a really bad storm. But the prayers to their false gods went unheeded. The storm intensified in spite of the prayers of everyone on board—everyone but Jonah, that is. That really perturbed the sailors; Jonah was asleep! "The captain went to him and said, 'How can you sleep? Get up and call on your god! Maybe he will take notice of us, and we will not perish'" (Jonah 1:6). "Do something to help out, Jonah!"

The situation worsened until the sailors decided the gods must be angry with one of them, so they cast lots to see which one it was. Naturally, God saw to it that the lot fell on Jonah.

So they asked him, "Tell us, who is responsible for making all this trouble for us? What do you do? Where do you come from? What is your country? From what people are you?" (Jonah 1:8).

Jonah told the truth about who he was and why there was such a storm. He knew God was disciplining him. I think Jonah knew Proverbs 3:11, 12: "My son, do not despise the Lord's discipline and do not resent his rebuke, because the Lord disciplines those he loves, as a father the son he delights in." If you drift away from God, he will let you go for a while, but there is going to come some discipline. Jonah was confident that he was being rebuked by God, so he recommended the sailors throw him into the sea.

To Jonah's credit, he was willing to sacrifice his own life so that these pagans could be saved. Jonah was a type of Christ even before he spent three days and three nights in the belly of the fish. The sailors, however, refused to throw Jonah overboard. At first, they tried everything they could to avoid it. They even tried to row back to land! But "the sea grew even wilder than before" (Jonah 1:13), so out of desperation the sailors finally tossed Jonah into the sea and asked God's forgiveness.

And the raging sea grew calm. At this the men greatly feared the Lord, and they offered a sacrifice to the Lord and made vows to him (Jonah 1:15, 16).

The Deliverance by a Fish

J. Vernon McGee says that one of the reasons he believes that this is a literal story is the graphic description of Jonah's experience of drowning in the sea.

You hurled me into the deep, into the very heart of the seas, and the currents swirled about me; all your waves and breakers swept over me. I said, "I have been banished from your sight; yet I will look again toward your holy temple." The engulfing waters threatened me, the deep surrounded me; seaweed was wrapped around my head. To the roots of the mountains I sank down; the earth beneath barred me in forever. But you brought my life up from the pit, O Lord my God (Jonah 2:3-6).

I once thought I was drowning. I was a junior in high school and had gone swimming in our neighbors' pond with their son, who was in college and much larger than I. We decided to practice saving somebody who was drowning, so I pretended I was drowning. I was in the middle of the pond, and he swam out to save me and grabbed me around the neck and started towing me to shore. What he didn't know was that he had my head under the water the whole time! I started scrabbling to get loose and he thought I was just playing along—struggling like a drowning person. He nearly drowned me trying to save me that day!

That is a petrifying experience. Jonah felt he was drowning, and he cried out to God for help. He was terrified. God could have let him drown. God could have raised up another prophet. "But the Lord provided a great fish to swallow Jonah" (Jonah 1:17).

Notice that word, "provided." This fish didn't just happen to be swimming by; it was there by a predetermined plan of God to accomplish His will. Nor does the Bible say it was a whale. Perhaps it was; perhaps it was not. Jesus identified it later as a "huge fish" Matthew 12:40). It seems to me that God created a special fish for this specific purpose—he "provided" it.

Jonah was inside this fish for three days and three nights. Talk about terrible accommodations! Imagine being bounced around inside that fish. That's the absolute worst place to be. "From inside the fish Jonah prayed to the Lord his God. He said: 'In my distress I called to the Lord, and he answered me'" (Jonah 2:1, 2).

Someone said that back when Hurricane Hugo was hitting Charleston, South Carolina, there was a group of Christians in a white board church who were praying like mad! The wind was howling outside when a man known for his eloquent prayers prayed out, "O God, send us the spirit of the children of Israel. Send us the spirit of the children of Abraham. Send us the spirit of the children of Moses. Send us the spirit of the children of the promised land!"

One guy interrupted him and said, "God, don't send no spirit, you come yourself. This is no time for children!"

Jonah also prayed to the Lord, and the Lord answered his prayer. "And the Lord commanded the fish, and it vomited Jonah onto dry land" (Jonah 2:10). The fish delivered Jonah to the shore so that he could travel to Nineveh. This was not only an unpleasant trip for Jonah, it wasn't very pleasant for the fish either. He probably preferred a school of blue gill. The fish became nauseated with this wayward prophet inside so he obeyed God's command and vomited Jonah onto dry land.

The Decision of the Ninevites

"Then the word of the Lord came to Jonah a second time: 'Go to the great city of Nineveh and proclaim to it the message I give you'" (Jonah 3:1, 2). It's not surprising that the next verse says, "Jonah obeyed the word of the Lord and went to Nineveh." Whatever was in store for him in Nineveh couldn't have been any worse than what he had just gone through, and Jonah didn't want to experience God's discipline again. He feared the discipline of the Lord more than the threats of the people of Nineveh. So Jonah went and informed the residents of Nineveh, "You are so wicked that, in forty days, this entire city is going to be history."

It is not surprising that Jonah obeyed, but it is surprising that Nineveh decided to repent. From the peasant on the street to the king in the palace, they put on sackcloths. They believed Jonah, and they repented of their sins. And no one was more surprised than Jonah.

Some people think that three days in the belly of this fish changed Jonah's appearance and ate away at his skin so much that, when he arrived in Nineveh and said, "I have been in the belly of a fish. God has spared my life, and I have come to you with a message from God," they believed him. They said, "You have been some place unusual!"

Jonah said, "If you don't repent, God is going to wipe out this city." So they repented, and God responded to their repentance.

> When God saw what they did and how they turned from their evil ways, he had compassion and did not bring upon them the destruction he had threatened (Jonah 3:10).

God spared the city, and Jonah, for whatever the reasons, was disappointed. Jonah said, "God, you have made me look like a false prophet, you've made me look silly." But God instructed Jonah that His grace reached not just to the Jews, but to undeserving Gentiles and even their animals.

Jonah 4:11 says, "But Nineveh has more than a hundred and twenty thousand people who cannot tell their right hand from their left." Now what does that mean? It could mean that they are spiritually blind. I take it there were a hundred and twenty thousand who were children. They were so young they did not know their right hand from their left. God said, "I am about to wipe out even their children. Don't you care about the innocent and many cattle as well? Should I not be concerned about that great city?" Psalm 36:6 says God preserves "both man and beast." And Ezekiel 33:11 says that he takes "no pleasure in the death of the wicked, but rather that they turn from their ways and live." I think there are three lessons about the nature of God that Jonah ought to have learned from the experience of being in the belly of the fish that we ought to learn, too.

The Omniscience of God

First he should have learned about the omniscience of God. So many times when we think about creation, we talk about the *omnipotence* of God. How powerful God is to create these mountains and this vast universe! We sing, "What a mighty God we serve," and, "Our God is an awesome God."

> O Lord my God! When I in awesome wonder consider all the worlds they hands have made, I see the stars, I hear the rolling thunder, Thy power throughout the universe displayed! Then sings my soul, my Savior God to Thee; how great Thou art.[9]

Indeed, God is a powerful God. But we need to think sometimes about the *omniscience* of God. His thoughts are higher than our thoughts. The brilliance of God ought to be noticed in his creation. How brilliant of God to design a bat with radar, a chameleon that can change colors, bears that hibernate and birds that migrate in winter, and animals that have incredible instincts from within! No wonder God looked upon the creation and said, "It is good." When God needed to transport Jonah across the water, he had the brilliance to create a special

[9]Stuart K. Hine, "How Great Thou Art," © 1953, renewed 1981, by Manna Music, Inc., 25510 Avenue Stanford, Valencia, CA. 91355. International copyright secured. All rights reserved. Used by permission.

fish to do the job. According to the *Encyclopedia Britannica,* man attempted for centuries to find some way to descend beneath the surface of the sea for scientific observation, to salvage wrecks, and to have an advantage in war. But the first mention of a craft that could be navigated under water did not occur until 1578. Submarines were not a major factor in battle until World War I, when Germany used them effectively. Two thousand years before man's mind was great enough to create a crude submarine, God provided a special fish to pick Jonah up and transport him from the ship he had boarded back to the land. What an awesome, mighty and omniscient God we serve.

The Sovereignty of God

Second, Jonah should have learned about the sovereignty of God. It was God's will that Jonah preach to Nineveh and that the people repent. One way or the other, God's will was going to be accomplished.

Leslie Weatherhead wrote a little booklet entitled, *The Will of God* that has really been helpful to me. In it he talks about God's will in three areas. First, there is God's "intended will." When he created this world, God created it intending it to be perfect—not tarnished by sin. Then there is God's "permissive will." Man in his freedom is able to disobey God and suffer the consequences of his sin. God does not interrupt the laws of nature to stop man's rebellion or to eliminate its results. Jesus stood over Jerusalem and wept saying, "It is my will that you would come to me as chicks gather under the mother hen's wings, but you would not." They were living in a permissive era of God's will. When a father gets drunk and abuses his child—that is not the will of God. God permits it, in that he does not interrupt the laws of nature and eliminate every sinner, but it is not his intent. Finally, there is the "ultimate will of God." Eventually, God's will is accomplished. Ultimately, in Heaven, he is going to put all his enemies under his feet.

Water provides a good illustration. Water in the Kentucky River is eventually going to flow into the Ohio River, into the Mississippi River, and into the Gulf of Mexico. A dam can be built to stop it temporarily, or it can be diverted, but ultimately that water is going to get to the Gulf of Mexico. It was God's intended will for Jonah to preach to the Ninevites. Jonah diverted God's will temporarily, but God through his discipline brought Jonah back to that very place where he accomplished his ultimate will.

Let me give you two examples from the Bible other than Jonah. One is Moses. It was God's intended will that Moses obtain release for the Hebrew slaves from Egypt. It was God's permissive will for Moses to disobey and murder the Egyptian. Maybe God intended for Moses to grow up in the palace and to sign a decree when he became Pharaoh. But Moses, in God's permissive will, rebelled. He committed murder, and God disciplined him for forty years in the wilderness. Ultimately, however, God brought Moses back to Egypt, and he led the people out in the Exodus.

A New Testament example is Saul of Tarsus. It was God's intended will for Saul to be His ambassador to the Gentiles. God gave him training and intellect. But Saul, in his defiance, refused to believe in Jesus. When Stephen, the first martyr, was stoned, they laid their garments at Saul's feet. Certainly the testimony and the preaching and teaching of Stephen should have converted Saul. But he was too rebellious, and his heart was too stubborn. So God disciplined him by striking him blind on the road to Damascus so that, ultimately, God's will was accomplished and Saul—better known as Paul—became the missionary to the Gentiles.

There is a key phrase in the record of Jesus' appearance to Saul on the road to Damascus. Jesus said, "Saul, Saul, why do you persecute me? It is hard for you to kick against the goads" (Acts 26:14). The "goads" were iron spikes that were put on a wagon right behind the legs of the oxen or the horses pulling the wagon. If the animals rebelled and kicked, they would kick against the spikes and injure themselves. God told Paul, "It is difficult when you rebel against me. You're kicking against the goads and hurting yourself. Ultimately, you're going to be submissive; ultimately, you're going to do my will." There is God's intended will, God's permissive will, and God's ultimate will.

Sometimes Christian people point to wrong decisions in their lives and say, "I think I've messed up God's will. I should have been a missionary, I should have been a school teacher, but I was too greedy, I wonder if I will ever be in God's will again." Well, if God has a specific assignment for you He is perfectly able to discipline you and bring you under submission. As Jonah picked the seaweed from his ear, I think he gained some respect for God's ultimate will, and he obeyed.

Please note, this does not eliminate our need to submit to God's will. For his ultimate will to be accomplished in us does require a spirit of submission on our part. He will not violate our own free will. If we pwesist in rebellion, he permits us to go our own way. Jonah repented and submitted to the Lord. Demas, on the other hand, "because he loved this world," deserted the apostle Paul and his mission (2 Timothy 4:9).

The Grace of God

There is one other thing Jonah should have learned about God: he should have learned about the grace of God. God gave Jonah a second chance when he didn't deserve a second chance. But what Jonah didn't understand was God was so full of grace that he was also going to give Nineveh a second chance. And when the people of Nineveh repented, God honored their change of heart and spared the city.

The Bible is full of examples of people who were given many chances by God—he is full of grace. Abraham, Jacob, Moses, David, Simon Peter, and Saul of Tarsus all made serious mistakes. But when they repented, God forgave them and used their service. He is full of grace and full of mercy. And God has given many of us a second chance, a third chance—a fifth chance.

When you discover God's grace—"While we were still sinners, Christ died for us" (Romans 5:8)—you say, "I'm approved. I'm already approved; I don't have to earn it. I don't have to pass a test. God approves me right now by the grace of the Lord Jesus Christ!" All that runs so counter to reason and so counter to our sense of justice that, if we don't study the Scriptural concept of grace, we gravitate to a legalistic mindset. As a result we can't win anybody. When we study the book of Romans, we say, "Christ died for us, His blood covers all our sins, and we are approved by God." Then we can come with a spirit of grace to other people.

When my older son turned sixteen and got his driver's license, I made a rule in our house. I said, "Anybody who gets a ticket in this house has to pay for it. You break the law—you find some way to pay." Sure enough, about three weeks after he got his license, his mother got a ticket! She didn't have the $125.00 to pay within ten days or go to jail, but love found a way. I said, "Tell you what, you are approved, I will pay. All you have to do is love me back."

God made a rule: "When you sin, you will die." We have all sinned, but, just as he did for Jonah, God gives us another chance and love finds a way. "For it is by grace you have been saved, through faith—and this not from yourselves, it is the gift of God—not by works, so that no one can boast" (Ephesians 2:8, 9).

Some time ago, Judy and I were in the home of Steve and Annie Chapman, singers from Nashville. On the wall we noticed a wooden dancing man—a wooden puppet with arms and legs that move. I remarked about it, and Steve said, "There is a story about that dancing man. You see, I grew up in a Christian home, but I really didn't understand. I had a legalistic mind-set, and I really rebelled against God and my parents. I went into a hippie life-style, and I really defied God. But when I came back, I started reading the Scripture. I was reading the book of Romans, and I came to understand God saved me by His grace. Because of the blood of Jesus Christ, I wasn't going to be accountable for my sins. I was free, I was approved by God. When that hit me, it hit me so suddenly I got up out of my chair and let out a war hoop and just danced around the room for about thirty minutes. I shared that in a church, and a woman made this dancing man for me. I put it in a frame and have it on the wall so that every time I look at it, I am reminded that I am saved by grace." I wonder if Jonah kept a little seaweed in his pocket to remind him he had been given a second chance. He, too, had been saved by God's great grace!

There was another man who rebelled against God—about 200 years ago. In his youth, he was a drunken defiant sailor. One day he got so drunk he fell overboard, and the only way they could rescue him was to harpoon him and drag him back. He was later saved by the grace of God. He was so overwhelmed by it that he wrote, "Amazing grace, how sweet the sound, that saved a wretch like me. I once was lost but now am found, was blind but now I see."

CHAPTER 6

Worry Is for the Birds!

Matthew 6:25-34

On a number of occasions I've asked people in Christian audiences to raise their hands if they struggle with worry. Almost always, about two thirds of those present will raise their hands and snicker a little about their open admission of worry. I then point out that they have just demonstrated that we consider worry a "respectable" sin. If I asked people to raise their hands if they had committed adultery or had taken God's name in vain the past year, I doubt anyone would raise a hand—even though there would undoubtedly be guilty persons present—and the atmosphere would not be frivolous.

Christians are willing to admit worry openly because they regard it as a "respectable" sin. Along with gossip and temper, it's a "weakness" that we're willing to confess, not a sin we keep hidden. In most people's understanding, anxiety is not on the list of the "ten most dangerous sins."

Jesus, however, saw it differently. Ten verses in the Sermon on the Mount are given to the subject of worry. Jesus made it clear that worry is a serious sin that needs to be properly diagnosed and cured.

Worry ruins our physical health. The Lord warned that in the last days "men will faint from terror, apprehensive of what is coming on the world" (Luke 21:26). The number-one killer in America is heart disease. A 1981 Associated Press survey suggests that 38% of deaths in America are the result of heart-related diseases—diseases brought on, the professionals say, by hypertension (high blood pressure) and anxiety.

Worry ruins our emotional stability. The number one prescription drug for over a decade was Valium, a tranquilizer for nerves. It has recently been replaced by Tagamet—a drug for ulcers. The suicide rate is up 100% in the last decade. Therapists are making a living trying to calm the fretful. We have all kinds of syndromes that are tension related: men in mid-life crisis, runaway wives, alcohol- and drug-addicted youth, insomnia, depression, and the list goes on.

Worry ruins our spiritual testimony. In Matthew 13:22, Jesus said the seed that fell among the thorns represents those who receive the word but "the worries of this life and the deceitfulness of riches choke it out, making it unfruitful." If one is burdened with worry, it becomes difficult to concentrate when he prays or worships, his witness is ineffective, his relationships are strained, and his gifts are stifled.

The Causes of Worry

Why is worry such a common problem today? Some of it has to do with our *temperament*. Some are sanguine temperaments who almost never worry. Pressure rolls off them like water off a duck's back. If things go well, fine; if not, they "stay loose" anyway. They are the kind of people who never get ulcers— they just give them to everybody else! Others are melancholy temperaments who, by nature, are perfectionists. They are sticklers for detail and agonize over small mistakes. Melancholy temperaments are wonderful administrators and are a blessing to any organization, but they are chronic worriers.

Another cause of worry is the *affluence* of our age. Solomon said, "The sleep of the laborer is sweet, whether he eats little or much, but the abundance of the rich man permits him no sleep (Ecclesiastes 5:12). It is erroneous to assume that the more material goods one has, the more secure he will feel and the less he will worry. Just the opposite is true: the more one possesses, the more he has to protect, insure, and worry about.

If I spend several thousands of dollars for a new Rolex watch, I have increased my potential for worry. If I play golf and hide the watch in the golf bag, I would keep a constant eye on the bag for fear someone might find it and steal it. If I walked through a dangerous section of town, I might pull my sleeve over the watch, for fear I might get mugged by someone wanting to steal the watch. When I went to church, I might be concerned that some Christians might consider me too materialistic since I owned such an expensive watch. Additional possessions can add to anxiety rather than decrease them.

I know of a college student who was given a Porsche by his father. After owning the beautiful car for just three weeks, he was playing softball when a sudden hailstorm sent all his friends scurrying for shelter. The young man who owned the car did not run for shelter, however, he dashed for his car and laid over it, trying to protect it from hail damage! Affluence can add to anxiety rather than decrease it. Solomon also said, "Being kidnapped and held for ransom never worries the poor man!" (Proverbs 13:8, *Living Bible*).

Another contributing factor to anxiety is *media hype*. We worry about matters to which people a century ago were oblivious. The media brings global problems right into our living rooms every night. We're informed about the trade imbalance with Japan, the federal deficit, the next nominee to the supreme court, and killer bees moving northward from Mexico. Not long ago, geologist Iben Browning predicted a major earthquake along the New Madrid fault. The newspapers and television stations promoted his predictions for weeks, and thousands in the midwest were anxious about the "big one" that was coming.

It's good to be informed, but one needs to remember that the media is in the business of improving ratings and selling advertising. One television newscaster admitted, "Our job is to keep your attention until the main event—which is, of course, the advertisement." In order to captivate attention, media personnel have to make whatever happens during the course of the day sound as threatening and crucial as possible, because if people don't watch, they don't sell ads; then they're out of business!

Imagine what would happen to the eleven o'clock news if nothing significant happened during the day. Would the newscaster on "Newsbreak at Ten" (or whatever they call the teaser to get you to stay up for the news one hour later in your area) say, "Folks, nothing really significant happened today. We're going to show cartoons at 11:00; we suggest you go to bed and get a relaxing night's sleep"? No! Whatever has happened during the day, regardless of how trivial, will be exaggerated in importance and made to sound ominous so you will stay up to watch the news.

Another factor that creates anxiety is *experience*. One might assume that the older we get, the less we worry. But the opposite is true: anxiety often increases with age because we have witnessed tragedies occur and we know terrible things can happen. A college student from our church went camping at Red River Gorge State Park in Kentucky. In the middle of the night, he wandered around and fell over a precipice and was killed. His parents were my age. They were devastated. I felt so sorry for them at the funeral. Now when my sons say, "We're going camping, Dad," I'll respond, "Be careful. Don't camp too near a cliff." They mumble, "Oh, Dad, you worry about the silliest things." But experience has a way of increasing anxiety. We know what can happen.

Erma Bombeck recently wrote an article entitled, "To Parent Is to Worry." I agree. One of the things that has surprised me about being a parent is how much I'm tempted to worry about my children now that they're older. I used to think that, once they were out of high school, the majority of my worries would be over. Not so! The anxieties of a parenthood seem to increase with experience.

Another factor contributing to anxiety is our *rapid pace of life*. Advanced travel, FAX machines, cellular telephones, and other modern "conveniences" have made our schedules so hectic that we seldom relax. We try to cram too much activity into every day. It's doubtful that God designed our nervous systems to cope with the kind of artificial pressures we place on ourselves. One man's tombstone read, "Hurried. Worried. Buried."

The primary cause of worry is *lack of faith* in God. Jesus said, "Oh, you of little faith." Man arrogantly wants to be in control of everything. He is determined to be in charge of his own destiny. He has a difficult time accepting any area of life that is beyond his ability to manipulate or direct. He's not willing to surrender significant areas to the providence of God. The Bible says, "Cast all your anxiety on him because he cares for you" (1 Peter 5:7). But too many people are not willing to take their burden to the Lord and leave it there. They want to be in charge themselves. So they spend a good portion of their time fretting over things that are beyond their control.

The Command: "Do not Worry"

Three times in this section Jesus commands, "Do not worry." What exactly does that command mean? I think there is a difference between *concern* and *anxiety*. Concern focuses on probable difficulties and results in action. Anxiety focuses on uncontrollable difficulties and results in inaction. Worry is always asking "What if? What if there is an earthquake? What if I get cancer? What if my son has an accident on the way home? What if my

78

company goes bankrupt? What if there is a war in the Middle East? Anxiety frets but takes no action; it focuses on problems that are beyond our control. Jesus said, "Don't be anxious."

But we need to be concerned. We need to give attention to real problems and seek to resolve them. Jesus said, "Consider the birds." I was watching a flock of birds one day. They were having a meeting in mid-October. Do you know what they were discussing? They were planning their upcoming trip to Florida! They sensed that winter was coming, and they were concerned enough to get ready to migrate. The Bible does not suggest a total disregard for tomorrow's potential problems. On the contrary, Jesus said,

> Suppose one of you wants to build a tower. Will he not first sit down and estimate the cost to see if he has enough money to complete it? For if he lays the foundation and is not able to finish it, everyone who sees it will ridicule him . . . (Luke 14:28, 29).

So it's not a sin to save for your children's education, to buy insurance or to plan ahead.

But we are commanded not to be anxious. Jesus said, "Who of you by worrying can add a single hour to his life?" (Matthew 6:27). Instead of increasing our life span, it decreases it. Worry is so futile—it accomplishes nothing.

Charlie Cullen suggested that, if we are going to worry, at least we ought to do it scientifically. First, write down all your worries. Transfer the anxiety from your mind to a piece of paper. Second, schedule a definite time every week as your "worry hour." Perhaps four o'clock Thursday would be a good time. Then, when the designated time arrives, sit down and start worrying to the best of your ability. If someone asks you what you're doing, just explain, "I'm going down my list of worries. I'm on number four now: the birth of my grandchild in four weeks."

"But," Cullen adds, "be sure to take your list with you, because you're going to look awful silly sitting there trying to remember what is was you were supposed to be worrying about!"

Somebody said, "Worry is enjoying a crisis before it arrives!"

In his book, *Now for Something Totally Different*,[10] Stuart Briscoe lists five things that Jesus said not to worry about.

[10]Stuart Briscoe, *Now for Something Totally Different: A Study of the Sermon on the Mount* (Waco: Word, 1978), pages 128-136.

First, don't worry about *finances*. Jesus said, "Do not store up for yourselves treasures on earth, where moth and rust destroy, and where thieves break in and steal" (Matthew 6:19). In other words, "Don't be anxious about your earthly possessions."

The *Book of Lists* catalogues "fear of financial failure" as the third most common apprehension of Americans:

"What if I can't pay off my credit cards?"

"What if my car breaks down?"

"What if interest rates skyrocket?"

"What if my investments collapse?"

Second, don't worry about *food*. We can easily understand why people in the first century worried about food. They were so poor they didn't know where the next meal was coming from. Today, we are blessed with food in abundance, but we spend so much time worrying about the content of food. I can't eat that—it has too much cholesterol, too much fat, too many calories. Don't eat sugar; it's bad for you. Watch out for Saccharin, it causes cancer. Take it easy on the salt, it increases blood pressure. Too much red meat isn't healthy for you. On and on it goes!

Third, don't worry about *fitness*, "about your body," Jesus said (Matthew 6:25). The body is, of course, the temple of the Holy Spirit (1 Corinthians 6:19), and it ought not to be treated like a garage! The Bible does say that physical exercise profits a little. But many Americans have gone to the extreme in their attention to the body. Aerobics classes, fitness centers, jogging shoes, health spas, weight lifting rooms, and exercise videos are raking in millions for their sponsors. Americans are consumed with their bodies. One's priorities are way out of balance when he spends several hours a day exercising the body but not five minutes reading the Bible and exercising the spirit.

Fourth, don't worry about *fashion*, "about clothes" (Matthew 6:28). That would also have been a natural anxiety of those living in the first century since they were so poor. Many owned just one garment, so clothing was a major concern. What if that one garment were torn? Then what? Most people today have an abundance of clothes, but they worry about fashion. Does it look right? Does it fit properly? Is this my color since I'm a winter? Does it clash with my shoes? Is this what others are wearing? Some will even phone in advance, "Are you wearing slacks or a dress?" "Are you wearing a tie or going casual?" People today worry about being in fashion.

Finally, don't worry about the *future*. "Who of you by worrying can add one hour to his life?" asked Jesus (Matthew 6:27). The fear of dying holds many in bondage (Hebrews 2:15), but even more than the fear of dying, many worry about aging. How they hate the signs that they're getting older. They get anxious about the little crows feet that appear around their eyes. They anxiously examine their faces for any new wrinkle and their scalp for any grey hair. They worry about balding and shifting body weight. They worry about the "major" birthdays: 30, 40, 50. They do their best to look younger—face lifts, tummy tucks, hair color, and more. Paul Harvey once told of a man who put braces on his false teeth so he'd look younger!

It's incredible! The very things Jesus said not to worry about are constant sources of anxiety for many.

The Cure for Worry

How can one win over worry? It's a serious sin that many of us commit daily. It's unrealistic to think that there is an easy cure. But Jesus said, "Look at the birds of the air" (Matthew 6:26). Several important lessons can be learned by observing the birds—lessons that will help to overcome anxiety. There is no magic pill, but there are some changes in attitude that once employed can really help to develop a spirit of calmness and peace.

Develop an Eternal Perspective

"Look at the birds of the air; they do not sow or reap or store away in barns, and yet your heavenly Father feeds them. Are you not much more valuable than they?" (Matthew 6:26) People are more important than birds because they have been created in the image of God, and God breathed into man "the breath of life." We have been promised eternal life.

> Are not two sparrows sold for a penny? Yet not one of them will fall to the ground apart from the will of your Father. . . . So don't be afraid; you are worth more than many sparrows (Matthew 10:29, 31).

The things of this world are critically important to the birds. Their primary focus is this world. But human beings are made for a higher purpose. We are special. We are spiritual beings. We should live with eternity in view.

Pagans who do not know God live for this world only. They chase after all these "things." But those who know the Lord should be constantly aware that "life [is] more important than food, and the body more important than clothes" (Matthew 6:25).

If a person knew that his house was going to burn down tomorrow, I doubt that he would spend today waxing floors, straightening the pictures on the wall, or painting the bedroom. He would remove from the house everything that was of value. Since we know that this world is one day going to be consumed with fire (1 Peter 3:10), our focus should be on those things that are eternal. The apostle Paul wrote, "So we fix our eyes not on what is seen but on what is unseen. For what is seen is temporary, what is unseen is eternal" (2 Corinthians 4:18).

One hundred years from now, it's probably not going to matter much that you were five pounds overweight, or that your child didn't make first team, or your wife put a dent in the fender of your new car, or whether people thought your tie didn't match your jacket. The things that will be important one hundred years from now will be matters of the heart, character, generosity, wisdom, gentleness, kindness, faithfulness, and the like.

A preacher related that he stopped and picked up a hitchhiker while traveling out of town. It was back in the late sixties, and the stranger was dressed as a hippie. He was very "laid back." When he came to an unexpected detour, the driver began to complain about the loss of time and inconvenience. The hitchhiker said, "Hey, man, don't sweat the small suff!" The preacher said that kind of became a motto for his life when he started to get uptight about something. "Don't sweat the small stuff!"

Almost everything about this life is "small stuff" compared to the things of eternity. It's not worth worrying about! Someone said, "The shortest distance between two points is always under construction!" If you are serene only when everything is going smoothly, you are going to live an anxious life. Peace of mind consists in large part from keeping eternal values in perspective.

That's one reason why we need to worship regularly. We go to church and are reminded that life is more important than food and the body more important than clothes and man is more important than the birds. We are able to realign our priorities and seek first the kingdom of God and His righteousness, knowing that all these things will be added to us. In worship, we turn our eyes upon Jesus, and we look full in His wonderful face. And the things of this earth do grow strangely dim in the light of His glory and grace.

Learn to Trust the Providence of God

A second lesson that should be learned from birds is to trust God's providential care. Jesus said, "Look at the birds of the air; they do not sow or reap or store away in barns, and yet your heavenly Father feeds them" (Matthew 6:26).

Probably everyone has heard it said of some petite person, "She eats like a bird." But there are some birds that eat two or three times their weight in food every day! If a human ate "like a bird," he'd be consuming 200, 300, maybe even 500 pounds of food every day. That would be some grocery bill!

But even though birds have to find so much food every day, they trust that God will supply their need. One seldom hears birds chirping in the middle of the night. They are sleeping. They don't pace their tree limbs worrying about whether there will be any worms, moths, or sunflower seeds to feed upon the next day. They are created to trust God's endless supply.

Birds do two things that humans would do well to emulate. They trust God to supply their need, and they work hard to assist him. Birds don't sit in the nest all day and expect God to drop food in their nests. Early in the morning they start looking. Birds trust, but they are diligent in searching for their needs to be supplied.

Trusting God doesn't mean laziness or indifference. It does mean realizing God is taking care of us. We've generally had enough to eat and something to wear. We've almost always had a roof over our heads. And even when we didn't, God got us through those hard times! If we make a reasonable effort, God has promised to provide for our needs. It's a matter of believing his promises and being content with what he has supplied.

That's what makes worry a serious sin. It is accusing God of being a liar. God says, "I will meet all your needs according to my riches in Christ Jesus" (cf. Philippians 4:19); worry says, "I don't believe he'll supply my needs. God promises in His Word, "In all things God works for the good of those who love him, who have been called according to his purpose" (Romans 8:28); worry says, "I don't believe things will work out for my good." God has said, "Trust in the Lord with all your heart and lean not on your own understanding; in all your ways acknowledge him, and he will make your paths straight"

(Proverbs 3:5, 6); worry says, "I don't believe God will direct my future." Jesus promised, "I am with you always" (Matthew 28:20); worry says, "I'm all alone."

God demonstrated his care for the children of Israel in one spectacular miracle after another.: the plagues on Egypt, the pillar of fire and the cloud to lead them, the parting of the Red Sea, water from a rock, the voice at Mt. Sinai, daily manna to eat. But when God commanded them to take the promised land, the Israelites were overwhelmed with anxiety. "They're giants! We're grasshoppers! We'll never survive!" they complained. God's anger was kindled against them because of their lack of trust. What more evidence did they need?

God has supplied our needs for many years. When do we become mature enough to conclude that his Word is true? He will supply our every need according to his glorious riches in Christ Jesus. I love that plaque that reads, "Lord help me to remember that nothing is going to happen to me today that you and I can't handle together."

Maintain Proper Priorities

Birds focus every day on the things of this world. Since humans are more valuable than birds, we are to "seek first the kingdom of God and His righteousness" and then the things of this world will be added to us. The Christian's priorities are God, people (with a special emphasis on family), job, and self. When one keeps these priorities in order, God promises to supply every need. But worry inverts priorities. The job becomes more important than family; self becomes more important than others. As a result, our responsibilities seem greater than our resources and our energy is sapped by anxiety.

When we trust God, we keep our priorities in order. We don't just say it; we do it. We go to church every Sunday even though it would be nice to have a weekend with the family on the lake. God comes first. We tell the truth, even though it would be to our financial advantage to lie. Others matter more than self. We put our work aside and listen to a spouse or child who wants to talk. Family matters more than the job. When we keep priorities in order, God supplies those things we need—especially peace of mind.

The professional golfer, Bobby Jones was known as a gentleman and a man of integrity. It is said that he was once addressing his ball in the rough when the head of his club touched a twig that jiggled the ball. Jones turned to his caddy and said,

"That will cost me a stroke." The caddy said, "Mr. Jones, I didn't see the ball move, and I'm sure no one else did." Bobby Jones answered, "I saw it move. I have to live with me." When a person lives a life of integrity, it eliminates so many anxieties because he is at peace with himself.

The word *peace* is used 220 times in Scripture, and it is often linked with the word righteousness. And righteousness always come first. "Righteousness and peace have kissed each other," the psalmist said.

Live One Day at a Time

Birds don't store up food in barns. They live one day at a time. "Therefore do not worry about tomorrow, for tomorrow will worry about itself. Each day has trouble enough of its own" (Matthew 6:34). The Lord was very practical. He didn't say, "Don't worry about tomorrow because nothing bad will ever happen to you." He was very realistic. He said there will be trouble tomorrow.

Bad things do happen in this world. The birds die. Sparrows fall to the ground. Tragedies happen to Christian people, too. Our parents get Alzheimer's. Our children have accidents. Our health breaks. Our companies go bankrupt.

Jesus said, "Each day will have trouble enough of its own." We are not promised exemption from problems, but we are promised enough spiritual resources to cope with them. Just as God provided just enough manna for the children of Israel to eat every day, so he will supply sufficient resources to meet daily stress. If today's problems measure a 6 on the pressure scale, he will supply six reinforcements. If they measure a 10 tomorrow, he will reinforce us with ten resources. But if we waste three of today's six resources worrying about tomorrow's ten pressures, we aren't able to stand up under the stress of today. We have to master the art of living one day at a time.

When Corrie Ten Boom learned that a friend had been persecuted for her faith in Christ, she was terrified. Corrie said to her father, "I will never be able to stand up under persecution. I couldn't take it."

Her father said, "Oh, yes, you can. If God allows you to be persecuted for His sake, you'll be able to do it."

"I just don't think I'm strong enough," she insisted.

Her father said, "Corrie, do you remember when you were a little girl and I took you to the train station? When did I give you the ticket? Remember how I waited until just before we boarded the train, and then I handed you the ticket? I had it in my pocket all along, but I waited to give it to you only when you needed it. God will be give you the resources that you need when the time comes."

Indeed. "God is faithful; he will not let you be tested beyond what you can bear. But when you are tempted, he will also provide a way out so that you can stand up under it" (1 Corinthians 10:13). Therefore, trust God to provide, and live one day at a time. Let the words of the psalmist be your motto: "This is the day the Lord has made; let us rejoice and be glad in it" (Psalm 118:24).

> Said the robin to the sparrow,
> "I would really like to know
> Why those anxious human beings
> rush about and worry so."
> Said the sparrow to the robin,
> "I think that it must be,
> That they have no heavenly Father
> Such as cares for you and me."[11]

---

[11]Elizabeth Cheney, "Overheard in an Orchard."

CHAPTER 7

Why Churches
Count People

Luke 15:1-10

A sheep is almost a defenseless creature. Rabbits can run away, skunks can emit a terrible odor, dogs can bite, horses can kick, and cats can scratch. But a sheep is nearly defenseless. It does not run fast; it can't bite hard; it doesn't have claws to defend itself; it can't burrow in the ground and hide. That's the reason sheep need shepherds. Most other animals can be left by themselves for a long period of time, but sheep need constant care and protection.

Instead of cooperating with the shepherd, however, sheep are often rebellious animals. You would think that such defenseless creatures would appreciate those protecting them, but they are too ignorant to know and admit they need assistance. They are unpredictable and untamable. That's the reason being a shepherd in biblical times was one of the lowest of all occupations.

When the Bible compares people to sheep, it is not a flattering analogy. Isaiah 53:6 says, "We all, like sheep, have gone astray." In the New Testament, Jesus is said to have looked upon the multitudes and had great compassion on them because he saw them as "sheep without a shepherd" (Matthew 9:36).

In the fifteenth chapter of Luke, there is a well-known parable about a sheep that got lost but was rescued by the good shepherd. The sheep was in such desperate straits that it gratefully submitted to the shepherd, who carried it home on his shoulders. Sheep can teach some very important lessons about the good shepherd's attitude toward the flock.

The Setting

There had been an accusation made against Jesus. "Tax collectors and 'sinners' were all gathering around to hear him. But the Pharisees and the teachers of the law muttered, 'This man welcomes sinners and eats with them'" (Luke 15:1, 2). Sinful people were very comfortable with Jesus. He was perfect, but His piety did not intimidate them. The woman at the well, who had been divorced five times; Zacchaeus, who was probably a cheater; the adulterous woman; and Mary Magdalene, who had been possessed of demons, all enjoyed Jesus' company. He did not condone their sin; he motivated them to change. Somehow they liked being around him, but the Pharisees and the teachers of the law were repulsed.

If Jesus really was the Son of God, they thought, He certainly would not cater to such an undesirable clientele! You know the slogans: "Birds of a feather flock together"; "You're known by the company you keep"; "Water seeks its own level"; "Bad company corrupts good character." I've used those slogans, too, and sometimes I sound more like the Pharisees than I do Jesus. When my son Rusty got married, one of his groomsmen had a ponytail. "A ponytail, Russ! What's happened to him?"

"Don't judge by appearance."

"I know, but that's a sign of rebellion." I sounded more like the Pharisees than I did Jesus. Some of you who have daughters are the same way. They bring home some young man from school they're dating, and you expect Prince Charming but he looks more like a clone of Axel Rose. You say, "Honey it's not Halloween. Who is this character?"

Our church has a program for teenagers on Wednesday nights. The program, called "Vision," is designed to reach unchurched teenagers. Several Wednesday nights ago, I spoke for the Vision program—they do attract young people who are not accustomed to church! Some of them are a little unkempt. Some of them, there for the first few times, may smoke outside the building. They get in the service and do not know exactly how to react.

Do they feel comfortable with us? A couple of them gave their lives to the Lord several weeks ago and were baptized. One came up out of the water and acted like he was strumming a guitar and said, "Excellent." If the church is the body of Christ, it should be a place where sinners feel comfortable and welcome, where they are motivated to change. The Pharisees were so proud of their piety that they could look down their noses at this group that Jesus had around him and say, "Oh they're sinners."

I grew up three miles outside of Conneautville, Pennsylvania. Conneautville is not exactly a big town. It has about a thousand people. It does not even have a traffic light. But some of the students in school who lived in town felt superior to those of us who were from the country. To them, we were "hicks." Of course, those same kids who looked down at us were considered to be "hicks" by kids from nearby Meadville, and the Meadville kids were "hicks" to the kids in Pittsburgh! It's ridiculous to look down your nose at somebody else. How ridiculous it must appear to God when one sinner looks down his nose at another. In fact, Romans 3:22, 23 reads like this: "There is no difference, for all have sinned and fall short of the glory of God." So, to illustrate His attitude towards sinners, Jesus told this story about the lost sheep. He said, "Suppose a man, a shepherd, has a hundred sheep. The shepherd counts the sheep as they enter the fold at night and he notices one is missing.

"What does he do? He leaves the ninety-nine safely in the fold and trudges over the dangerous countryside until he finds that one lamb that is lost. He finds that little lamb, perhaps snagged in a bush on the mountainside; he lifts it onto his shoulders, and he carries it back to the fold.

"When he gets back, he calls his friends and neighbors together and says, 'Rejoice with me! I have found my lost lamb.' And they rejoice with him."

Most Christians know that story like the backs of their hands, and that version is what they know. But there are three mistakes in that story.

Number one, the shepherd did not leave the ninety-nine *in the fold.* We get that idea from an old song. "There were ninety and nine that safely lay in the shelter of the fold." Remember that old song? But that's not what the Scripture says. "Does he not leave the ninety-nine—" Where? This is in Luke 15:4: ". . . in the open country." The shepherd took a risk leaving the ninety-nine out in the open, but he was so concerned about the lost that he took the chance that maybe somebody could attack the ninety-nine.

I sometimes hear Christians say, "I think we ought not to put so much emphasis on evangelism and start nurturing the people we already have." The Bible does say that we ought to teach those who have been baptized. I hear people say, "We shouldn't be out there building a new building so we can bring more in; we ought to give attention to edifying the ones we have now." But the Lord is primarily concerned about the one who is not a part of the flock, the one who is lost without a shepherd. The church that focuses only on feeding its own flock will experience decline.

Our first commission is to evangelize. The church is the only institution I know that exists primarily for the benefit of non-members. Christians never grow faster, and are never nurtured more, than when they look out and try to bring somebody else in.

The second error in the story above was that the lost animal was a *lamb*. You have seen that painting of the shepherd leaning over the edge of the cliff to pull the little lamb out of the snag. That's a moving picture, but the Bible doesn't say it was a lamb that got lost. It was a sheep.

One might ask, "What difference does it make?" It would make a big difference if you had to carry it home! A little lamb is pretty light but not a sheep. A sheep may weigh anywhere from 100 to 250 pounds! It took a tremendous amount of effort for this shepherd to find and then lug that sheep home.

The Bible says that when Jesus died, the Good Shepherd, God, "laid on him the iniquity of us all" (Isaiah 53:6). That was a very heavy burden! Effective evangelism is not easy. It takes work and diligence and sometimes perspiration. When churches enter into big building programs, they are taking on themselves a lot of effort and sacrifice. Why bother? Because those churches care about people who are lost!

The third mistake in the story was that *the neighbors rejoiced* with him. They may have—but the Scripture does not say they did. Normally a shepherd would corral his sheep at night. When he counted them, he found out one was missing and went out, evidently in the dark. It had to be late when he came back. I imagine all the neighbors and friends were in bed. He said "Come on out and rejoice with me." I can hear someone say, "We are glad you found your sheep, but tell me about it in the morning." You see, for the neighbors to rejoice, they would have to share the passion of the shepherd. But that was the point of Jesus' parable. Those who really know the shepherd rejoice when he rejoices.

My wife, Judy, was telling me about a mother who had been shopping at a wholesale store. Her little baby was in the cart, and she took her eyes off the baby for several seconds. When she looked back, the baby was gone. She looked around and did not see anybody holding the baby, and she panicked. She raced to the security guard at the door and told him what had happened. The security guard immediately got on the PA system and announced some kind of emergency code. Nobody could leave the store. They began to search all through the store, and they found the baby abandoned in the rest room—already sedated so as not to cry. Apparently, the abductor had heard the code, recognized it, and fled.

When I told this story to my congregation, there was noticeable rejoicing when I said the baby was found even though the people did not even know the mother or the baby's name. But they know a mother's passion, and they know the preciousness of a baby! They breathed an audible sigh of relief when they learned the baby was found. Now Satan has snatched God's children and numbed them with the propaganda of this world. When one child is found, the Bible says, Heaven rejoices. If we care about people, and we know anything about the mind of God, we will have the same passion he has; we rejoice when one is snared from the evil one. Jesus said, "I tell you that in the same way there will be more rejoicing in heaven over one sinner who repents than over ninety-nine righteous persons who do not need to repent" (Luke 15:7).

The Permissiveness of God

From this parable, four facts can be learned about God. First, observe the surprising permissiveness of God. When the sheep wandered away on its own, the shepherd let it go. The shepherd was not negligent; the sheep was just wayward.

God created man with freedom of will. Man can choose to accept or reject, to follow or to drift away. When we choose to wander away from God, he lets us go. We are not on a leash that he yanks every time we make a mistake or drift away. The Good Shepherd leads by example, but if his sheep are too ignorant to follow, he lets them learn the hard way.

King David is a good example of this. When he invited Bathsheba to come to the palace for a visit, he was drifting from God's will, but God did not strike the palace with lightning. He let David go. After David committed adultery with Bathsheba and she became pregnant, God did not afflict David with leprosy. He let David try to weasel his way out on his own. When David tried to arrange for Uriah to come home so he could cover up the deed, God didn't stop David. When David plotted

Uriah's death and then married Bathsheba for himself, God did not strike David blind. He let him go. The former shepherd strayed so far away that eventually he knew he was desperately lost. The man after God's own heart had chased after Satan's fantasy, and he knew he needed help. We talk a lot about God's sovereignty—"God rules," "God's in charge,"—and that shows us his greatness. Another aspect of God that shows his greatness is his tremendous patience and permissiveness. Even though he could stop us, he lets us go. The reason he does this is that he doesn't want begrudging obedience, like a slave in shackles. He wants our volunteer affection, like a servant on his knees. God gives us freedom to wander, and then he patiently waits for us to return.

There is another story in Luke 15. It's about the prodigal son. When I heard that story as a boy, I often thought the father of the prodigal son was too permissive. He should not have let the boy go; he should have said, "No, you can't have your inheritance. You have to stay home and work." But the father of the prodigal son permitted his boy to wander off because a restrained rebel is worse than a wandering sinner. The rebellion intensifies, but the sinner is going to hit rock bottom. Bishop Fulton Sheen used to say, "God prefers a loving sinner to a loveless saint." He lets us wander for a time hoping that we will want to return on our own and we will be submissive.

The Concern of God

The second thing to observe in this parable is the individual concern of God. The shepherd had a huge flock. It has been suggested that a normal flock would be about thirty sheep. This guy had a hundred sheep. He was overburdened, but he still counted every one. I sometimes hear people say, "The church shouldn't be concerned about numbers." That is foolish. If the church cares about people, she is going to count. Somebody in the Bible counted: twelve disciples with Jesus; one hundred and twenty in the upper room (Acts 1:15); three thousand converted on Pentecost (Acts 2:41); five thousand men later (Acts 4:4). Another book in the Bible is called Numbers.

If you care about people, you count. This shepherd counted his sheep and discovered one was missing. Notice that he didn't say, "Well I've got more than I can handle anyway; you've got to expect to lose a few along the way." He was concerned about the one that was lost. God has nearly six billion people in the world. That's a lot of people. You know how many a billion is? A billion seconds ago, John F. Kennedy was inaugurated. A billion minutes ago Jesus Christ walked on the face of the earth. A billion hours ago man did not exist. A billion dollars ago was about yesterday noon in Washington, D. C. So a billion is a lot and that's a difficult number to fathom.

We are assured in Scripture that even though there are almost six billion people, God cares about every one of us individually. He notices even when a sparrow falls.

My parents had six children. Even though they had six, I think they loved each of us equally. Still, I remember one time we were half-way home from church and somebody counted noses, and my brother was not in the car. Then they remembered that John was asleep on the pew back at church and they had just forgotten him. My mother didn't say, "Well, we have five; that's enough. Let's go on home." She could not get back there fast enough—and there he was, kind of ticked off. She embraced him and told him that everything was okay.

We all know that parents have the capacity to love more than one child, and the Father God has the capacity to love each of us individually. God does not love Billy Graham or Mother Teresa more than he loves you. Isn't that amazing? I like the story of Zacchaeus. As Jesus was traveling through Jericho, he was surrounded by admirers, curiosity-seekers, and that despised little tax collector sitting in a tree. It amazes me that Jesus noticed him with all those people. Even more amazing is that Jesus knew Zacchaeus by name. He had never met him. "Zacchaeus, come on down, let's do lunch today over at your house." Isn't that amazing? Imagine how that made Zacchaeus feel!

I remember being down on the floor at a Kentucky Colonels basketball game years ago. I had gone down to see Donny Beckhart, a member of our church, who was running the clock. As I was talking to Donny, somebody yelled at me from the floor and said, "Hey Bob! Hey Bob!" I looked up, and there was Dan Issel, star player of the Colonels, calling my name. It really made me feel important—Dan Issel knew my name.

I wonder how Zacchaeus felt—Jesus called him by name. That amazes me because there are so many people I can't call by name. I should, but I can't. I want to tell you that God knows your name. When God called Samuel, just a young boy in the tabernacle, he called him by name: "Samuel, Samuel." Jesus Christ knows you by name. Not only that, he knows the number of hairs on your head. He knows the thoughts of your heart. He knows your needs even before you ask. Isn't that amazing? The individual concern of the Father shows us his greatness.

The Pursuit of God

The lost sheep also illustrates the aggressive pursuit of God. He "goes after" the lost sheep. The word for *goes after* suggests untiring persistence, a tenacity. God is permissive enough to let you wander, but he is compassionate enough to come searching for you if you don't return.

When Adam sinned, God came into the garden and said, "Where are you Adam?" God let David drift for about a year. When David didn't come back on his own, God came searching through a prophet by the name of Nathan. Nathan told David, "You have sinned, David, and God loves you too much to let you get by with it."

When you see somebody you love getting caught up in alcohol or drugs or deviant behavior, what do you do. If you love the person, you get together with some of his friends, and you plan to intervene. As a group, you call this person in and you say, "I love you too much to let you continue in this behavior. I want you to know that you're really hurting me and you are hurting yourself. Would you go to a clinic for treatment?" That is a tense meeting—as you well know if you have ever participated in one. I have. But you do it anyway because you care too much to let that person continue to wander away! When we rebel against God, he lets us go for a while, but he loves us too much to let us continue to destroy ourselves. Eventually, he comes calling.

David wrote, "Where can I go from your Spirit? Where can I flee from your presence? If I go up to the heavens, you are there; if I make my bed in the depths, you are there" (Psalm 139:7, 8). You never get so far away that God can't come calling.

Frances Thompson wrote a book about God's search for man. He called it *The Hound of Heaven*. Perhaps you have children who have drifted away, and there is nothing you can do except pray for them. God loves them too much to let them continue to go without confronting them. It may be a Gideon Bible in a motel room; it may be the rebuke of a friend; it may be an automobile accident; it may be a tremendous blessing; it may be a hymn on the radio. But you can count on it. He will not let you be comfortable in sin for very long. Jesus said, "I came to seek and to save that which was lost."

The Joy of God

Finally the lost sheep teaches us about the ultimate joy of God. The shepherd was elated when he found the lost sheep, and he joyfully put it on his shoulders and went home. Do you ever think about God celebrating and laughing, or is your image of him always one scowling and ready to discipline people for their sin? Jesus said the shepherd joyfully puts the sheep on his shoulders and comes back and asks his friends to rejoice with him because he has found the lost sheep. God wants his church to be concerned about the lost and to pursue and rescue them and then rejoice when they are found.

Tony Campolo wrote an interesting book about the church; he calls it *Party Time.* That describes something of what the church should be: a celebration. In our church, we are privileged to witness people almost every week come to know Jesus Christ. Some churches see it once a year—or even more rarely than that. I wish everyone could be down front when people come forward. Some come to move their membership; some have wandered away for a while and are coming back. But those who come to give their life to Jesus Christ sometimes make the most inspirational statements. They will say: "I want to give my life to Jesus"; "I have waited long enough"; "It's time for me to be a Christian"; or "Thank you for teaching me about the Lord." After church, the friends or family members of those who have come forward will come up and say, "Oh, I'm just so happy about So-and-so's coming today. We have been praying for them. We have invited them, and it's just so great."

This passage says, "I tell you that the angels of heaven rejoice when one sinner repents." There is a European legend about a shepherd who lived in the mountains with his daughter. When she was a little girl, she loved to go out in the pasture with her father. She particularly got a thrill out of hearing him call the sheep with that loud distinctive shepherd's call that would echo through the mountains. The legend has it that she got older and very beautiful and moved to Glasgow. She wrote fewer and fewer times and began to live a fast, loose life. The father heard a rumor that his daughter was not living as she had been trained. With a broken heart he went down into the streets of the city. They said it was really a sight to see this man in a shepherd's garb carrying a staff going into some of the dives of the city asking about his daughter. He could not find her, but he refused to give up.

One morning he said, "I know what I'll do, I'll call to her with the shepherd's voice." He walked the narrow streets of that city calling out, "Mary! Mary! Mary!" And in some dingy apartment, she faintly heard that call. She pushed aside her companion and went to the window and saw her father coming down the street. She ran down to meet him, and he embraced her and loved her. He took her back home and nursed her into right living. The legend says that on the mountainside there is a gravestone over that girl's body that has etched on it one word: *forgiven*.

Maybe you have wandered some and drifted. I want you to know the Father loves you too much to let it go on very long and right now he is pursuing you. Maybe you can hear his still small voice calling your name.

CHAPTER 8

Who's a Chicken?

Matthew 26:31-35; 69-75

"You're chicken!" As a boy growing up on the farm, I hated those words. If somebody were to say, "You're a chicken if you don't jump off this beam into the hay mow," that was a challenge. Of course, I would jump. I had to prove I was no chicken.

When I played high school football, I was a very small quarterback; I weighed 140 pounds. I never would have put it this way then, but I became kind of a "chicken quarterback." When I went back to pass, I could unload a pass pretty quickly if delay meant taking a hit by a 200-pound lineman at the last second.

Don Loni, a popular youth speaker, tells about the last play he participated in in football. He was running with the ball, he said, when a big lineman grabbed him by one leg and a big linebacker grabbed him by the other leg. One pulled in one direction and the other pulled in the other direction and said, "Make a wish buddy; you're going for a ride." He decided that it was better to be a chicken than a wishbone and then he quit.

Foolish teenagers used to play a game called "Chicken." Two automobiles would line up facing each other about a quarter of a mile apart and pick up speed as they headed right toward each other. The first one to swerve to get out of the way was "chicken," and the one who stayed the course was the winner. What a ridiculous game! In reality, anybody who would be foolish enough to try a stunt like that would have to be pretty insecure and fearful to try to impress his peers.

People will go to ridiculous lengths to avoid being labeled a chicken because a chicken is a fretful bird. It is easily frightened and always runs from confrontation. To call a human being a chicken is to label that person a coward, afraid to do anything daring.

The Bible relates an incident where a chicken confronted and convicted a disciple of Jesus. Matthew 26 recounts how a rooster reminded Peter of his sin and motivated him to repent. Of course, the rooster didn't deliberately confront Peter, but its crowing at the appropriate moment caused Peter to realize he had been a chicken—he had been cowardly in his faith. A careful study of the story will teach some lessons that can help modern disciples avoid a similar offense.

The story begins with Jesus' giving a warning to the disciples in the upper room. Matthew 26:31: "This very night you will all fall away on account of me, for it is written: 'I will strike the shepherd, and the sheep of the flock will be scattered.'" Now why did Jesus say that? Doesn't that sound like negative thinking? Jesus wanted his disciples to understand that he understood their weaknesses. He anticipated their failures. Going into a state tournament game, a basketball coach may tell his players, "You're going to walk into that big arena and you're going to be nervous. You're going to miss some shots that you wouldn't normally miss." The coach will try to prepare the team for the inevitable and help them to recover as quickly as possible. The coach is saying, "It is normal to be nervous; don't panic when it happens. Just regain your composure and play your best." Jesus knew that the pressure of the next twenty-four hours would be more than the disciples could stand. They would run for their lives, but he was encouraging them, "When it happens, regain your composure and come back."

Peter, however, objected to any suggestion that he would act cowardly. He declared, "Even if all fall away on account of you, I never will" (Matthew 26:33). Simon Peter had a touch of Barney Fife in him—and a little bit of Ralph Kramden. They kind of overestimate their own strength. You love them for their transparency and honesty, or for their humanness, but they overestimate their own ability. So Jesus gave a very specific prediction to Peter.

> "I tell you the truth," Jesus answered, "this very night, before the rooster crows, you will disown me three times."
>
> But Peter declared, "Even if I have to die with you, I will never disown you." And all the disciples said the same (Matthew 26:34, 35).

This was no shallow boast. Peter really meant it. He was carrying a concealed weapon, and he was ready to fight for Jesus. He was determined not to fall. Luke's Gospel records that Jesus said, "Simon, Simon, Satan has asked to sift you as wheat. But I have prayed for you, Simon, that your faith may not fail" (Luke 22:31, 32). Twila Paris sings, "Deep inside this armor the warrior is a child." Peter was a warrior; he had his sword ready. But Jesus knew that, in his heart, like every person, Peter was just a child. Peter went on to deny Jesus. He just did not understand how relentless and insidious Satan's attack would be.

"Now Peter was sitting out in the courtyard, and a servant girl came to him. 'You also were with Jesus of Galilee,' she said" (Matthew 26:69). The disciples had all fled when Jesus was arrested, but Peter turned around and followed Jesus at a distance. He crept right into the courtyard outside the high priest's residence, where Jesus had been taken. That took a measure of courage, a fact that is sometimes overlooked in discussions of this incident. Mark 14:54 says, "He sat with the guards and warmed himself at the fire." Peter made a major mistake, one that a lot of us make: he tried to attack Satan on Satan's own territory.

Years ago in Waynesville, North Carolina, on a golf course, I saw a dog make that mistake with a duck. A dog chased a duck on the shore and the duck immediately scrambled into the water and started to swim away, but the dog chased after the duck, trying to swim after it. Big mistake! The duck was cruising along and the dog was scrambling for his life to catch up with him. If the duck got too far away, she would wait until the dog would almost catch up. Then the dog would start paddling, going wild and the duck would cruise away and wait and sometimes would just go down under the water and disappear. That old dog was looking around and the duck would reappear about twenty yards away. He would paddle after her right out into the middle of the lake, and then she disappeared. I saw that dog's head go lower and lower as he began to get exhausted. He scrambled with all his might and crawled up on shore and panted and looked over at that duck. He couldn't believe it. He almost lost his life.

The dog could chase the duck and win on shore, but the water was the duck's territory. Peter went into enemy territory, and he wasn't ready to cope with it. Satan had him right where he wanted him.

We do the same thing. "Mom, I know that she's not a Christian but I think I can date her and change her."

"I know that movie has really bad language but it has some good content and I don't have trouble with that language. I can go."

"I know there will be a lot of drugs and drinking going on, but I'm able to cope with it. I'll go to the party."

"I go to the track frequently, but I don't have a gambling problem. I just love to see the horses run. When they come down the final stretch, I just praise God for these great creatures that he has made."

"I disagree with some of the doctrine they teach, but I'm learning about meditation and I think that will be helpful for me."

"I'll miss a lot of church with this job, and I'll have to be gone on weekends, but I'll listen to you on tape."

Peter thought his faith was strong enough to withstand any temptation, but he was warming himself at the devil's fire. He was trying to attack Satan in his territory, but suddenly the courageous disciple turned chicken.

> A servant girl came to him. "You also were with Jesus of Galilee," she said.
> But he denied it before them all. "I don't know what you're talking about," he said (Matthew 26:69, 70).

The Bible says, "If you think you are standing firm, be careful that you don't fall" (1 Corinthians 10:12). Peter thought he was a man of courage, but he denied the Lord so quickly he must have been stunned at what he had done. Maybe he rationalized that he was an undercover agent and, after all, you've got to lie on occasion to get the insider information.

> Then he went out to the gateway, where another girl saw him and said to the people there, "This fellow was with Jesus of Nazareth."
> He denied it again, with an oath: "I don't know the man!" (Matthew 26:71, 72).

One thing is almost always true of sin: it's easier the second time. And sin almost always intensifies, too. This time, Peter not only denied Jesus, he denied with an oath. "I was never with him. I swear to God—I don't even know who he is."

After a little while, those standing there went up to Peter and said, "Surely you are one of them, for your accent gives you away."

Then he began to call down curses on himself and he swore to them, "I don't know the man!" (Matthew 26:73, 74).

The Galileans spoke with a particular brogue. Just as people from Massachusetts or eastern Kentucky are often recognized by their accents, so a Galilean would sound different from most people in Jerusalem. Some of the people in the courtyard noticed this, and they called him on it. What else would a Galilean be doing in the high priest's court if not to see what would become of his Galilean friend?

Peter was really chickening out by this time. He not only denied Jesus, he not only lied with an oath, he called down curses on himself to prove his lie. "May God strike me dead if I'm not telling you the truth! I never have associated with Jesus of Nazareth. I have never met the man."

The last phrase of Matthew 26:74 reads "Immediately a rooster crowed." Luke's Gospel records that, just as the rooster crowed, "the Lord turned and looked straight at Peter" (Luke 22:61). Peter didn't realize that, when he spoke that last oath, Jesus was being escorted to another trial. He lifted his eyes and caught the disappointment in the look of Jesus, who had just heard him. Suddenly Peter realized what he had done and was crushed. He remembered the words of the Lord "and before the rooster crows you'll disown me three times." He went outside and wept bitterly.

I grew up in a great Christian home. One thing we were taught was never to swear. That was one of the worst things one could do. I fouled out of an eighth-grade basketball game once, and we lost. In the locker room, I threw my shoe up against a locker and lost my temper and swore. A teammate said, "Hey, guys, did you hear that? Russell swore." I did not even know they noticed. What was more disappointing, I looked up and saw that my dad had just walked into the locker room. I saw a look of disappointment on his face as he turned and walked out. I had not only violated God's Word and hurt my testimony, I had disappointed my dad, whom I deeply loved.

When I read this story, even though that incident occurred thirty-five years ago, I remember it almost every time. I wonder if Peter remembered what he had done every time he heard a rooster crow. The rooster's crowing convicted Peter of his sin. The rooster was not doing anything unusual, it was just doing instinctively what God had created it to do. But by doing what it normally did, it served the purpose of God.

When we live as God intends for us to live, He uses us to influence people even when we are not aware of it. You may think nobody notices your language and whether or not you take God's name in vain, but they notice. You may think your neighbors don't notice when you go off to church on Sunday morning. They casually wave when you come home and drive into your driveway, but your behavior and your consistency with what God has instructed you to do convicts them. You regularly pray before meals, pay your bills on time, or give to causes that stop at your door. Your children notice, and they will remember.

One Mother's Day, my son Phil gave a testimony about his mother. He said, "I can never remember my mother watching a soap opera, but I remember a lot of times, when I came downstairs in the morning, she was reading the Bible." She didn't even know that he noticed.

We are always looking for some dramatic way to serve God. We long for some moment when we'll know that we have accomplished something spectacular. God often uses his people in routine, unspectacular responsibilities. We may not know until eternity the impact that our lives have had on somebody who has observed us. That is the reason the Bible says, "Let us not become weary in doing good, for at the proper time we will reap a harvest if we do not give up" (Galatians 6:9).

The rooster crowed as it did every morning. God created it that way. But that morning, that routine reflex was used by God to remind Simon Peter of his error. I can see four important lessons that Simon Peter should have learned from the crowing rooster.

God's Warnings Are Always True

It happened just exactly as Jesus said it was going to happen. The Bible warns us repeatedly about the terrible results of sin. God's warnings are always true.

"The wages of sin is death" (Romans 6:23).

"Righteousness exalts a nation but sin is a disgrace to any people" (Proverbs 14:34).

"The one who sows to please his sinful nature, from that nature will reap destruction" (Galatians 6:8).

"If you keep on biting and devouring each other, watch out or you will be destroyed by each other" (Galatians 5:15).

"Sin . . . easily entangles" (Hebrews 12:1).

"Your sin will find you out" (Numbers 32:23).

"Their [false] teaching will spread like gangrene" (2 Timothy 2:17).

"The pleasures of sin [are] for a short time" (Hebrews 11:25).

"Watch out for those who cause divisions and put obstacles in your way" (Romans 16:17).

"Wine is a mocker and beer a brawler; whoever is led astray by them is not wise" (Proverbs 20:1).

All of these are warnings, and they always come true.

I watched a news clip once about a local high-school girl who was killed in an automobile accident. There had been a party; there had been warnings not to drive, but they did anyway. The driver hit a tree and was seriously injured and the passenger was killed. The next day, four or five teenagers gathered around the tree where their friend had died and left flowers and mementoes. The news reporter asked one of the teenagers, "What have you learned?"

She said, "We've learned it is dangerous to drink and drive."

I was glad she learned that, but I wondered about all those warnings: "Don't drink and drive." "Friends don't let friends drive drunk."

Why does it have to hit so close to home before we learn the lesson? Why can't we read it in God's Word and understand God's warnings are always true? And what about this one? "Righteousness exalts a nation but sin is a disgrace to any people." When the angel came to Sodom and Gomorrah and warned that God was going to destroy that city by fire and brimstone, the people scoffed. Only Lot and his two daughters escaped. Now we have the warnings. Arnold Toynbee, imminent historian, says of the twenty-one major civilizations in history that he studied, nineteen collapsed from within. Yet educators, politicians and the media continue to scoff at the prophets of God today who are warning that, if we continue in indulgence and immorality and greed, this nation is bound for collapse. Righteousness exalts; sin is a disgrace. Yet the warnings go unheeded.

Peter heard the rooster crow and he knew God's warnings are always true.

Everyone Has Limitations

A second lesson Peter should have learned was that everyone has limitations. E. Ray Jones, a preacher in Clearwater, Florida, said, "We have a tendency to overestimate our ability to cope with temptation and underestimate our ability to cope with suffering." We see somebody going through horrible suffering and we say, "Oh, I could never go through that." But if we faced that suffering, the Holy Spirit would lift us up and we would be able to go through it. We overestimate our ability to handle temptation. Simon Peter said, "I'll never deny you. I'll die for you." He was so confident he marched right into the devil's territory.

When we overestimate our strengths, we let down our guard and give Satan a foothold. Gordon MacDonald is a well-known Christian author and preacher. Some time ago, he got caught up in a series of bad decisions and poor moral choices that nearly cost him both his ministry and his family. To his credit, he openly admitted his sin and repented of it. God has restored him, and today he has an effective ministry and is still writing books and touching people's hearts. The irony is, his failure came in an area in which MacDonald believed he was "safe." The "bottom line," MacDonald said, is this: "An unguarded strength and an unprepared heart are double weaknesses."

A few years ago I gave a speech at a college commencement. Before the festivities began, a member of that school's board sat with me in the president's office. We'd never met before, and we were asking questions of each other that might help us get better acquainted.

Suddenly, my new friend asked me a strange question. I've thought about it many times since then. "If Satan were to blow you out of the water," he asked, "how do you think he would do it?"

"I'm not sure I know," I answered. "All sorts of ways, I suppose; but I know there's one way he wouldn't get me."

"What's that?"

"He'd never get me in the area of my personal relationships. That's one place I have no doubt that I'm as strong as you can get."

A few years after that conversation my world broke wide open. A chain of seemingly innocent choices became destructive, and it wasa my fault. . . . And then my world broke—in the very area I had predicted I was safe.[12]

The Bible says, "If you think you are standing firm, be careful that you don't fall" (1 Corinthians 10:12). There are four

[12]Gordon MacDonald, *Rebuilding Your Broken World* (Nashville: Nelson, 1988), pp. 47, 53.

areas of temptation where men are most likely to fall. These areas are sex, sloth, silver, and self. I asked the men in a men's fellowship group once to visualize those four words and, in their minds, to circle the one that they thought was their greatest area of weakness. Then I asked them to circle in their minds the one that they thought was their greatest area of strength. Then I said, "In your mind, you have just circled the two areas where you are most likely to fall. The one is a character weakness, and you recognize it. The other is an unguarded strength. That's the area where you get careless and Satan may attack you from behind."

I think David would have listed sex as a weakness because he had a weakness for lust, but he would have listed sloth as a strength because he was a hard working shepherd and king and an ambitious soldier. But it was in a time of leisure, when others were going off to war and he was strolling on the housetop that he fell. Peter was so confident of his loyalty to Jesus that he would attack with a sword. But in that very area in which he thought he was strong, he became weak. An unguarded strength became a double weakness. That is the reason Stephen Brown said, "We ought to always pray for the strong because they are weak."

Sin Always Brings Pain and Misery

A third lesson Peter learned was that sin always brings pain and misery. He had denied Jesus because he didn't want to experience the pain of rejection, but sin did not bring escape or satisfaction. He went out and wept bitterly. Satan cleverly presents sin as attractive. Charlie MacMahan is a young preacher who participated in my son's wedding. He told that he and his wife, Sherry, went out to eat and the waitress came by and listed the desserts that were available. One of them was called "sin's delight." His wife immediately said, "Oh, that sounds good!"

Sin does sound good. Satan is able to package it in such attractive paper, but, as somebody said, "All Satan's apples have worms." The members of the House of Representatives took advantage of special banking privileges and bounced checks. It was such a little violation, such a convenience. Who would know? But their sin found them out and now there is so much backlash that many of the worst offenders lost their seats by the next election. Sin's delight becomes sin's distress, and that's true with every sin.

Failure Is Not Final

One final lesson that Peter learned is the most important one. When he heard the rooster crow, he began to learn that failure doesn't have to be final. Peter made a major mistake. He delighted the enemies, disappointed Jesus, and devastated himself. He ran out of the courtyard and began to weep. I don't think Peter got over that quickly.

There is a legend that says when Peter was older, as he went through various towns, the enemies of Christ would wait until he was off in the distance and would mimic the sound of a rooster crowing to remind Peter of that day he had been a chicken. But Peter began to discover that failure doesn't have to be final. God honored his repentant spirit. Psalm 51:17 says, "The sacrifices of God are a broken spirit; a broken and contrite heart, O God, you will not despise." Isaiah 66:2 says, "This is the one I esteem: he who is humble and contrite in spirit, and trembles at my word." When Peter went out and wept bitterly, the Holy Spirit began to work in his life and gave him another chance.

After the resurrection, Jesus cooked a breakfast for some of the disciples. Sitting around the fire, he looked at Simon Peter and said,

"Simon, . . . do you truly love me more than these?"
"Yes, Lord," he said, "you know that I love you."
Jesus said, "Feed my lambs."
Again Jesus said, "Simon, . . . do you truly love me?"
He answered, "Yes, Lord, you know that I love you."
Jesus said, "Take care of my sheep."
The third time [was it because Peter had denied him three times that Jesus asked him to confess three times] he said to him, "Simon, . . . do you love me?"
Peter was hurt because Jesus asked him the third time, "Do you love me?" He said, "Lord, you know all things; you know that I love you."
Jesus said, "Feed my sheep."

Jesus did not just forgive Peter; he did not just reinstate him. He gave Peter the opportunity to be the primary spokesman on the Day of Pentecost. He gave him the keys to the kingdom of God. When God forgives and gives a person a second chance, he gives that person a wholehearted second chance. Peter learned that a failure isn't final.

One morning I walked through the Wayside Mission in Evansville, Indiana. They reach out to the homeless and needy in the city. There I met a man named Bill, and he said, "For twenty years I was on cocaine. I had no place to come. I came to this place and I found Jesus." The director said that Bill had been working at a packing company and had just received a promotion. The Lord has given him a dramatic second chance.

I also met Jerry that morning. The director said, "Jerry, do you have a word of testimony?"

Jerry said, "I always do." He said, "I came here on drink. My mind was messed up, but I gave my life to the Lord 'cause I had nowhere else to turn. I was baptized and now I'm working here as a cook. I'm so happy." He said, "I don't have nothin', but I've got him."

As Christians, we are all people of a second chance—and a third chance. We need to learn, with Peter, that there can be a devastating mistake, a terrible failure, but the Lord will still be there asking, "Do you love me? Then feed my sheep."

CHAPTER 9

The Kosher Question

Acts 10

My little-league baseball coach was a black man by the name of Paul Jones. Paul was a popular and admired figure in our little community. He had been an outstanding high-school athlete but had contacted polio shortly after high school and became paralyzed in his left arm. He would pitch batting practice to us with one arm. For fielding practice, the catcher would toss the ball to him and, with one hand, he would be able to direct where he wanted to strike the ball. Paul never seemed bitter about his handicap. He was jovial, friendly and very well liked. He had two sons and two nephews who were about my age. We played on the same team for a number of years and developed a good friendship through little league and Babe Ruth baseball.

I think that the Lord used that experience in my life to help prevent racial prejudice. I guess nobody could say that he does not have any prejudice at all, but I don't think racial prejudice has been a problem for me. Part of the reason for that is that I learned to respect and appreciate Paul Jones and his family.

But, from time to time, other kinds of prejudice has surfaced in my life. For example, when I hear there has been a plane crash overseas and 200 people have been killed, and then I hear the reporter say, "But no Americans were on board," I breathe a sigh of relief. And then I think, "Why, those people that were killed are just as valuable in God's sight as Americans. Each one is somebody's mother or father or sister or brother or child." And I feel ashamed.

At the end of the Persian Gulf War, I found myself being very thankful that there were so few casualties. Less than 200 American soldiers and pilots lost their lives in Operation Desert

Storm. That was wonderful! I believe it was an answer to prayer. But I don't like to think about the several hundred thousand Iraqi soldiers who were killed. I don't like to see those pictures of vehicles that had been bombed on the highway leading out of Kuwait and the horror of those Iraqi soldiers and their families. Nationalist pride has its place, but, as a Christian, I have to grow to see the world the way God does. God is not sitting in heaven with an American flag draped around His shoulders celebrating all of our victories. He is as concerned about his people in Asia, Africa, Australia, and Europe as he is about those in the United States. I need to go back and remember that song, "Jesus loves the little children, all the children of the world. Red and yellow, black and white, they are precious in His sight. Jesus loves the little children of the world."

Simon Peter needed to learn that lesson, too. Peter was Jewish, and he loved the Israelite nation. He took pride in the fact that the Hebrews were God's chosen people. At Philippi, Jesus had told Peter, "I will give you the keys of the kingdom of heaven" (Matthew 16:19). Peter had used those keys on the day of Pentecost, when he stood up in front of all those Jewish people and began his sermon by saying, "Fellow Jews and all you who live in Jerusalem, . . . listen carefully to what I say" (Acts 2:14). God used Peter's sermon to touch people's hearts, and he was gratified to see 3000 Jewish people come and accept Jesus as Savior.

What Peter didn't know was that those keys were to be used to open the doors for the Gentiles to enter the kingdom as well! Peter considered the Gentiles spiritually inferior and excluded from the grace of God. It would take divine intervention for him to preach the gospel to the Gentiles. It was not something he would do naturally. In a sense, Simon Peter was a religious bigot, but he became the first to communicate the gospel to the Gentiles in spite of his prejudice. The story is found in Acts 10, where the Holy Spirit can be seen breaking down barriers and expanding the disciple's horizon. The account teaches many lessons about seeing the world from God's perspective.

The Praying Gentile

The story begins with a Gentile by the name of Cornelius. "At Caesarea there was a man named Cornelius, a centurion in what was known as the Italian Regiment" (Acts 10:1). Cornelius was a man who made the military his career. A centurion was, of course, a man who was in charge of 100 soldiers. Interestingly, almost every centurion mentioned in the Scripture is described in a favorable way. In Matthew 8 there is a centurion who came to Jesus asking Jesus to heal his son, "But you don't have to come to my home," he said; "just give the order." Jesus said, "I've not seen so great a faith, no not in all of Israel." It was a centurion who stood at the foot of the cross and was so impressed with Jesus' death that he said, "Surely this man was the Son of God" (Mark 15:39).

This centurion, named Cornelius, was a good man, too. "He and all his family were devout and God-fearing; he gave generously to those in need and prayed to God regularly" (Acts 10:2). Cornelius was conscientious. He prayed regularly, gave generously, lived morally. People sometimes ask, "What will happen to good moral people who have never had the chance to know Jesus Christ?" I think the Bible teaches that a perfect God is going to judge them by their available light. One of the things I see in Scripture is that, if people really search after God, he gives them additional light. Jeremiah 29:13 says, "You will seek me and find me when you seek me with all your heart." Cornelius was seeking God, and he was about to be found.

"One day at about three in the afternoon he had a vision. He distinctly saw an angel of God, who came to him" (Acts 10:3). God spoke to people in those days in a variety of ways: through a voice, a burning bush—and here Cornelius saw an angel. The angel said, "Send men to Joppa to bring back a man named Simon who is called Peter. He is staying with Simon the tanner, whose house is by the sea" (Acts 10:5, 6).

The Prejudiced Christian

This was going to be such an unlikely meeting that there had to be divine intervention. That introduces us to the second character in the story, Simon Peter who was a prejudiced Christian. All his life, Simon had believed that the Jews were God's chosen people. They had the truth, the Old Testament law. They had the physical sign of obedience, circumcision. The Jews had the dwelling place of God, the temple. And the Jews had the promise of God, the coming Messiah. All his life, Peter had believed that Gentiles were spiritually inferior.

On a visit to Boston one summer, my wife and I noticed this sign at a delicatessen across from Harvard University: "Harvard chicken, a degree above the rest." The Jewish people felt like that—a degree above the Gentiles. So the Gentiles were not permitted into areas of the temple that were restricted. A law-abiding Jew would not eat with a Gentile and certainly would not go into his house. Some rabbis went so far as to say a Jew should never help a Gentile woman give birth to a child because she was helping give birth to another sinner who was going to be fodder for hell.

These basic concepts were etched deeply into Peter's mind, and it was not going to be easy to change them. The church was about eight years old at this time, and every Christian was Jewish or a Jewish proselyte. In Peter's mind, the Messiah had come for the Jews. In spite of that mind-set, Peter is the one to whom the angel directed Cornelius to send his messengers.

"About noon the following day as they were on their journey and approaching the city, Peter went up on the roof to pray" (Acts 10: 9). In those days the houses were small, and the rooftops flat. They provided something of a patio where one could go for privacy. On the roof, Peter became hungry and wanted something to eat, but the noon meal was still being prepared.

While on the roof, Peter fell into a trance. A very important truth was about to be communicated to Peter. His consciousness was heightened to receive this vision from God.

> He saw heaven opened and something like a large sheet being let down to earth by its four corners. It contained all kinds of four-footed animals, as well as reptiles of the earth and birds of the air. Then a voice told him, "Get up, Peter. Kill and eat."
>
> "Surely not, Lord!" Peter replied. "I have never eaten anything impure or unclean" (Acts 10:11-14).

The Jews had strict laws against eating certain kinds of animals. The book of Leviticus details which kinds they were. Jews were permitted to eat any animal that had split hooves and chewed the cud. Thus, they could eat beef, lamb, and venison but not other kinds of animals such as pigs, camels, or rabbits. They were not to eat creatures in the sea that did not have fins and scales, so they could not eat catfish or lobster. They were not to eat most birds, eagles, hawks, or ravens. Bats were unclean. They were not to eat flying insects. They were permitted to eat locusts, katydids, and grasshoppers.

These laws were given to maintain the distinctiveness of the Jewish race. Some people think they were also given to help with their health. Mickey Smith, who for many years was a missionary to Indonesia, said that one of the toughest things he ever had to eat was dog. In Indonesia, dog meat is considered to be a delicacy. He said the bad part was, when people who ate dog meat started to perspire, they would smell like dogs! We are repulsed by that idea, but that is exactly the way the Jews felt toward the Gentiles' practice of eating pork and catfish and other unclean foods. It was repulsive to them.

The voice of God spoke to him a second time, "Do not call anything impure that God has made clean" (Acts 10:15). This happened three times, and then the sheet was taken back to Heaven without any further explanation. Peter was uncertain about what this vision meant. One usually learns best what he has to think about and discover on his own.

> While Peter was still thinking about the vision, the Spirit said to him, "Simon, three men are looking for you. So get up and go downstairs. Do not hesitate to go with them, for I have sent them" (Acts 10:19, 20).

This is not a coincidence, this is a "God-incidence." Just then there was a knock on the door. Peter answered it and discovered two soldiers representing Cornelius. They related how their commander had been told by an angel to send for Simon Peter because he would have a message for them.

"Then Peter invited the men into the house to be his guests" (Acts 10:23). Peter was taking the first step in accepting Gentiles. A rigid Jew would not invite a Gentile into the house, but Peter's attitude was beginning to soften. He was becoming more tolerant. I am sure some of Peter's rigid friends thought he was becoming liberal, but he was becoming more Christlike.

The Providential Encounter

Cornelius was waiting for Simon Peter. Excitedly, he called together his family and close friends. When Peter entered the house, Cornelius met him and fell on his face as though to worship Peter. Peter said, "Don't worship me. I'm just a man like you." (See Acts 10:23-26.) How unlike some modern Christian leaders who want people to fall at their feet or put them on a pedestal! Peter went inside and found a large gathering of people (Acts 10:27). When he saw all these Gentiles jammed in the house it must have immediately conjured up the image of the sheet jammed with unclean beasts. Suddenly the meaning of the vision became clear. He could hear God's voice as he looked at these Gentiles, "Don't call unclean what I call clean."

Peter was not very tactful in his approach. I spoke in a church in Newport News, Virginia, once, and an elder in the church came up to me later and said, "Do you know Wayne Smith from Lexington?"

I said, "Yes I know him well."

He said, "He was here last year, and he really did a good job. You're good, but you're not as good as he was!"

Now that is not very tactful, that's not what a guy wants to hear. Peter met all these Gentiles, and he was equally tactful.

He said to them: "You are well aware that it is against our law for a Jew to associate with a Gentile or visit him. But God has shown me that I should not call any man impure or unclean. So when I was sent for, I came without raising any objection. May I ask why you sent for me?" (Acts 10:28, 29).

That doesn't seem to me to be the polite thing to say. "I don't want to be here; I've never been in a Gentile house before, and I hope you don't contaminate me. God told me to come here." Cornelius, a gracious man, apparently wasn't offended. He just explained his visit from a angel, concluding with these words:

So I sent for you immediately, and it was good of you to come. Now we are all here in the presence of God to listen to everything the Lord has commanded you to tell us (Acts 10:33).

This is a preacher's dream! Some Christian people have heard the gospel so many times that they are always listening with a critical ear, ready to find some doctrinal deviation. And then there are some pagans who are so hard-hearted that their ears are stopped up and one has to work for their attention. Any preacher would love to have someone say, "We're just here to listen to whatever you have to say—we're not in any hurry." That's one of the reasons I like to teach the "What We Believe" class at our church. Many times there are people in the class who don't know much about the Bible or the Lord and are hungry and eager to learn. They are not in a hurry to move on to the next activity. Peter welcomed this opportunity.

"Then Peter began to speak: 'I now realize how true it is that God does not show favoritism but accepts men from every nation who fear him and do what is right'" (Acts 10:34, 35). Then he told them about Jesus Christ! He told them how God had anointed Jesus with the Holy Spirit and power, how he went around doing good and healing people, and then how he was killed by crucifixion and was then raised from the dead on the third day.

> While Peter was still speaking these words, the Holy Spirit came on all who heard the message. The circumcised believers who had come with Peter were astonished that the gift of the Holy Spirit had been poured out even on the Gentiles. For they heard them speaking in tongues and praising God (Acts 10:44-46).

"The Holy Spirit came on them," Peter said later, "as he came on us at the beginning [on the Day of Pentecost]" (Acts 11:15). This was a final confirmation to Peter that this was the exact meaning of the vision he had had the day before. The Gentiles were not to be considered unclean beasts. They didn't have to become Jews before accepting Christ. The gospel was for them, too. Jesus died for them as surely as he died for the Israelites.

> Then Peter said, "Can anyone keep these people from being baptized with water? They have received the Holy Spirit just as we have." So he ordered that they be baptized in the name of Jesus Christ (Acts 10:46-48).

By the way, if someone didn't need to be baptized it would have been Cornelius. He was devout, believed in the Lord, was baptized in the Holy Spirit, and spoke in tongues. All that confirmed to Peter that this man was to be accepted. Peter said, "All right, the first thing he needs is to be baptized in water." That shows how important it was. This is the first Gentile admitted to the kingdom of God. It resulted in considerable controversy among the Jewish Christians. Simon himself would wrestle with this issue again, but he learned from the vision of unclean beasts that God does not show favoritism. The gospel of Christ is for everybody.

The Personal Application

We don't wrestle with this Jew/Gentile question anymore, but there are two lessons from Peter's vision that Christians today should learn. First, *all foods are declared clean*. There are some believers today who say Christians should honor the Old

Testament diet restrictions. Some Christians are vegetarians and suggest that we should refrain from eating meat altogether. I talked with a man the other day who said, "When I eat a fish, I feel guilty. I feel like I'm eating a friend." Jesus didn't feel that way. In John 21, Jesus cooked fish for breakfast, and he ate it with his disciples.

In Mark 7:18, 19, Jesus made it clear that all foods are to be considered clean.

> "Don't you see that nothing that enters a man from the outside can make him 'unclean'? For it doesn't go into his heart but into his stomach, and then out of his body." (In saying this, Jesus declared all foods "clean".)

There are some foods that I find objectionable because of their taste and content. I don't like liver or gizzards. I'm not crazy about cow's tongue, chitlins, pig's feet, or oysters. In Africa I ate zebra and crocodile meat. The worst thing I ever ate was buffalo meat. Someone gave us buffalo meat once, and it looked and tasted like shoe leather. I haven't had a craving for chocolate covered grasshoppers for a long time! But those foods are not unclean. The people who eat them are not sinful—they just have weird taste. It's probably better to avoid fatty and high cholesterol foods and red meats most of the time, but those things are a matter of diet, not of faith.

Some may conclude that they are healthier for being vegetarian. That's fine. But they ought not to impose that as a Christian standard on anyone else because it's not in the Bible. Colossians 2:14 informs us that Christ has canceled the Old Testament code with its regulations that were against us. He nailed it to the cross. Verse 16 says, "Do not let anyone judge you by what you eat or drink, or with regard to . . . a Sabbath day."

So all foods are clean. And if you're weird enough to eat some of those things, that's okay. You'll just go to Heaven quicker than some of us!

The second lesson is the more important one, and that is that *all people are loved by God.* Jesus modeled this attitude in John 4 when he spoke with the Samaritan woman. He was talking to a woman, to a woman of another race, and to a woman with a horrible background. She had been married five times and was living with a man to whom she was not married. John 4:27 says,

Just then his disciples returned and were surprised to find him talking with a woman. But no one asked, "What do you want?" or "Why are you talking with her?"

The disciples kept their prejudice to themselves, as we often do, but deep inside they felt it just wasn't right. They probably hoped something like this would never happen again and that no one would see Jesus doing it. Just then the woman at the well ran off to tell everyone she could what had happened.

Jesus said to the disciples, "Do you not say, 'Four months more and then the harvest'? I tell you, open your eyes and look at the fields! They are ripe for harvest" (John 4:35). The disciples saw the woman at the well and her associates as unclean. Jesus saw them as loved and He desired to have them as part of His kingdom.

What do you see when you look at a person who has been divorced five times? Do you snub your nose at them and keep them at arm's length, say "Unclean"? Jesus sees them as people who need his love, his forgiveness, and his renewal. He did not come to call the righteous but sinners to repentance.

When an unmarried couple who are living together comes to church, how do you respond? Do you say, "Unclean! I don't know why they are here? What are they trying to prove?" Or do you say, "Good, I hope they will hear and understand the gospel and allow Christ to change them." Jesus said, "The well do not need a physician, but the sick do."

What's your reaction to a person who is homosexual? Do you treat him or her with disdain, make sarcastic remarks, "Unclean"? Or do you think to yourself, here is someone who really needs Jesus Christ. If he would just surrender his life to the Lord, the Lord could transform his desires and his life-style. Jesus said, "Come unto me all who are weary and heavy laden, and I will give you rest."

Do you not know that the wicked will not inherit the kingdom of God? Do not be deceived: Neither the sexually immoral nor idolaters nor adulterers nor male prostitutes nor homosexual offenders nor thieves nor the greedy nor drunkards nor slanderers nor swindlers will inherit the kingdom of God (1 Corinthians 6:9, 10).

We would like to stop right there. We don't want to know what the next verse says.

And that is what some of you were. But you were washed, you were sanctified, you were justified in the name of the Lord Jesus Christ and by the Spirit of our God (1 Corinthians 6:11).

The Corinthian church was made up of recovering alcoholics, prostitutes, and homosexuals who had been changed by Jesus Christ. What do you see when you see an AIDS patient? Does your heart hurt for that person? Are you anxious to make sure he is ready to meet the Lord? Or do you think, "Unclean! He got what he deserved." What do you see when an interracial couple moves next to you? Do you look at them with contempt? "How could they do that to their children?" Or do you conclude that those are people who need Jesus Christ just as much as you do? When someone comes into church who is not dressed well or whose mannerisms are not cultured or whose attitude is sorry, how do you react?

Adolf Coors IV spoke at our church once and gave a great testimony. I went out with him afterwards, and he talked about how he got rid of the family business and is not associated with the distillery anymore. He also told me that he speaks to some Christian groups where people will come up to him afterwards and say, "What right do you have to talk about Jesus Christ? Your brewery has destroyed more families and has hurt more lives than anyone I know of." Unclean!

Some time ago I was sitting in the sanctuary about half-way back. During the Communion service, I looked up and saw a young man in his early twenties standing at the pulpit just looking out. I thought, "That's not an usher—and I don't think we have a guest speaker." One of our men, Todd Barton, quickly went over and had a talk with him. The young man said, "This church is such an awesome place, I just wanted to see it from up here." He was so high on drigs, he didn't know up from down. Do we say, "Get him out of here. Unclean"? Or do we say, "Let's get him some medical and spiritual help"?

I got a note on a roll call card one Sunday from a first-time visitor. It read, "We sat in traffic for ten minutes and walked three blocks only to be told by a parking attendant, we should have parked and taken a bus. What a miserable experience." My first reaction is to write back and say, "What a sorry attitude. I've gone to ball games, paid to park, walked six blocks, and been happy to be in the crowd. Love Jesus!" It's like Yogi Berra said about a restaurant, "It's so crowded nobody goes there anymore."

But in reality, the person who wrote that note needs Jesus Christ. If he is already a Christian, he needs to grow in grace. The fruit of the Spirit is patience and joy. If he is not a Christian, he needs Christ to transform him to the point where he can say, "It was so good to be in the house of the Lord even though it is crowded." But it takes a while to get to that point, and our attitude toward those people is very important to their getting there.

Do you see people as Jesus sees them? He sees them the same way he sees you; as sheep having no shepherd; as sinners who need forgiveness. Becky Pippert spoke to a women's retreat our church sponsored and told about a girl who asked to see her in private after a book-signing session. The girl was crying, and she said, "Years ago, my fiance and I were youth leaders in a very large, influential church and were kind of the darlings of the church. We won hundreds of young people to the Lord and everyone loved us. In our relationship, we became sexually involved." She said, "You can't imagine the spiritual schizophrenia of trying to encourage young people to be pure while at the same time utterly compromising ourselves.

"In the course of time, I became pregnant. We just couldn't tell the church. I mean, we didn't think the church could handle it. There had never been a scandal. We were so ashamed, we took what we thought at the time was the easy way out, and I had an abortion. That was ten years ago, and my husband was able to receive the forgiveness of God. I thought I knew the Scriptures about forgiveness, but I just can't accept it, and I feel awful. I cannot believe what I have done. My wedding day was the worst day of my life. Everybody was smiling as I came down the aisle, yet a voice kept saying, 'You are a murderer. You have taken an innocent life. How could you do such a thing.'" She broke out in tears and said, "I just can't believe I was capable of doing such a horrible thing!"

Becky Pippert waited to say what was on her mind because she wanted to make sure it was the right thing. Finally she said to the girl, "You know, you may be surprised that you are capable of murder, but I'm not surprised—because that's not the first murder you've committed. You know you murdered the innocent Son of God? Jesus Christ died on the cross because of your sins, and you helped to murder him. Martin Luther said, 'We carry in our pockets his very nails.'"

The woman stopped crying and said, "You know, you are right. What you are telling me is that I just poured my heart out to you, telling you the very worst thing I've ever done. I can't get over it, but you are telling me I've done something worse. And that's right, I shouldn't be surprised that I'm capable of such a sin because I've already done something like that."

Then she said, "Becky, if God can forgive me for helping kill Jesus, there is nothing He can't forgive me for, is there?" And Becky Pippert said, "What God reveals through the cross is that we are far worse then we ever imagined and yet forgiveness is offered to us." When you look at the cross you see your sinfulness. The Bible says, "There is no difference, because all have sinned and fall short of the glory of God, and are justified freely by his grace through the redemption that came by Christ Jesus" (Romans 3:22-24). When we understand ourselves, that we are not innocent, how can we call anybody "unclean"?

When Jesus died on that cross, there was an inscription over his head that read, "King of the Jews." It wasn't just written in Hebrew, it was written in Greek and Latin because Jesus died for the sins of the whole world. He died for everyone who hurts. There is no one unclean, no one not welcome in the kingdom of God. That's what the church is about, that Jesus came for sinful people like us.

CHAPTER 10

Strange Bedfellows

Isaiah 11:6-9

The wolf will live with the lamb, the leopard will lie down with the goat, the calf and the lion and the yearling together; and a little child will lead them (Isaiah 11:6).

I once heard about a zoo that had a very unusual exhibit. A lion and a lamb inhabited the same cage. They could be seen lying peacefully side by side. Observers were amazed that the ferocious, carnivorous lion and the passive, helpless little lamb could co-exist. When pressed, the zoo keeper explained, "It's our most popular exhibit. And it's not really that difficult to maintain. . . . Of course, I do have to replace the lamb every three or four days!"

The animal kingdom is a hostile, violent kingdom. There are natural enemies: snakes and rodents, birds and insects, cats and mice, foxes and chickens, sharks and fish, leopards and goats, the lion and the lamb. These are adversaries. That's just the way things are.

Isaiah predicted that, when the Messiah established his eternal kingdom, all violence and hostility would end. "The cow will feed with the bear, their young will lie down together, and the lion will eat straw like an ox" (Isaiah 11:7). The animals that are carnivorous will become vegetarian in the messianic kingdom.

Not only will the wolf lie down with the lamb and the lion and the yearling live at peace, but little children will be unharmed as they play with formerly ferocious animals.

The infant will play near the hole of the cobra and the young child put his hand into the vipers nest. They will neither harm nor destroy on all my holy mountain, for the earth will be full of the knowledge of the Lord as the waters cover the sea (Isaiah 11:8, 9)

A Prophecy of Eternal Life

This passage is a prophecy about eternity. Isaiah predicted that there will be no adversaries in Heaven.

When studying Bible prophecy, one needs to remember that prophecy can be literal or figurative. For example, the Old Testament predicted that the Messiah would be born in Bethlehem (Micah 5:2). That was fulfilled literally. But the Old Testament also predicted that Elijah would prepare the way for the Messiah (Malachi 4:5, 6). That was fulfilled figuratively by the ministry of John the Baptist.(Matthew 17:10-13). So when studying Bible prophecy, it is important to avoid dogmatism and maintain flexibility.

Some believe that there will be animals in God's eternal kingdom, and those animals will be restored to the nonviolent spirit that was present in the garden of Eden before the fall. They will live in peace. Romans 8:20-22 says the creation was "subjected to frustration" because of sin. The whole creation groans at present because of its distorted purpose. But the creation has hope that one day it will be liberated from its bondage to decay and be brought into the glorious freedom of the children of God.

But Isaiah 11 carries an important application for our edification and our hope: when God's kingdom is established in perfection, the hostility between human beings will end and people will live at peace with one another.

> In the last days. . . . He will judge between the nations and will settle disputes for many peoples. They will beat their swords into plowshares and their spears into pruning hooks. Nation will not take up sword against nation, nor will they train for war anymore (Isaiah 2:4).

Heaven is going to be a place of spiritual peace. Men will not make war against Jesus Christ any longer. Every knee will bow and every tongue will confess that Jesus Christ is Lord. Jesus is the Lion of Judah. He has the power to destroy and devour helpless human beings. People are like sheep who have all gone astray (Isaiah 53:6). But the Lion and the lamb will be together in harmony. Christ in his love and mercy forgives. Man in humility and repentance worships. And there will be peace.

122

Heaven is going to be a place of *relational peace*. "He will settle disputes for many peoples." The Christian Arab and the Christian Jew will be at peace. Democrat and Republican Christians will be at peace. The Washington Redskins and Dallas Cowboy fans who belong to Christ will be at peace! The blacks and whites, rich and poor, young and old, environmentalists and industrialists will not train for war anymore. Even some husbands and wives who have battled each other for years will experience harmony for the first time in the eternal kingdom.

Heaven is going to be a place of *personal peace*. The apostle Paul admitted to an internal civil war. He said, "For I have the desire to do what is good, but I cannot carry it out. For what I do is not the good I want to do; no the evil I do not want to do—this I keep on doing" (Romans 7:18, 19). Every believer knows the constant battle against temptation and sin. Every Christian has suffered an occasional defeat and can testify to the frustration and disappointment that follows. But the wonderful thing about Heaven will be that the war will be over. The victory will have been achieved."He will wipe every tear from their eyes. There will be no more death or mourning or crying or pain, for the old order of things has passed away" (Revelation 21:4) There will be peace.

Christian people really need the constant hope of Heaven. That daily anticipation helps us persevere in difficult times and appreciate the good times on this earth.

Suppose a cruise ship in the Caribbean is overtaken by hijackers. The leader gleefully announces the takeover on the public address system and states that if their demands are not met in three days, the ship will be blown to pieces. "In the meantime," the hijacker sneers, "the restaurants will still serve food, the dance band will still play, the casinos will still be open, the pool is still available—have a good time!"

I doubt if people on board that ship would have much fun. Everyone would be focused on the potential disaster. But if the ship's captain suddenly came over the P.A. system and said, "Ladies and gentlemen, this is your captain speaking. I have great news! The hijackers have been arrested and taken into custody. We will continue the cruise as planned, and we will anchor in four days in Miami. Have a good time!" That announcement would be followed by an ecstatic celebration. Everyone would rejoice, and every minute of the cruise would be appreciated even more.

In order to enjoy the present, there must be an end in view. Paul told Titus that our faith rests "on the hope of eternal life, which God, who does not lie, promised before the beginning of time" (Titus 1:2). He told the Romans, "May the God of hope fill you with all joy and peace as you trust in him, so that you may overflow with hope by the power of the Holy Spirit" (Romans 15:13)

A Demonstration by First-Century Believers

This passage in Isaiah is more than just a prophecy about the eternal kingdom. It's God's intent for the church. Jesus Christ is the Prince of Peace. When He rules in the hearts of people, hostility is broken down and former adversaries live in harmony.

Jesus' twelve disciples form kind of a microcosm of the church. The handful of disciples that Jesus selected to be his associates contained some natural adversaries.

Take Simon the Zealot and Matthew for example. Simon was a political right-winger—a redneck conservative of the first century. He belonged to a group who advocated the violent overthrow of the oppressive Roman government. The Zealots hated all Romans and made no bones about it. They were sometimes called "dagger bearers" because they carried concealed knives and swords and would seek opportunities to stab a Roman soldier when he was isolated in a secluded alley or jostled about in a crowd. The Zealots fought guerilla warfare. They burned, looted, and vandalized Roman-occupied buildings. They did everything they could to make life miserable for the foreign troops and officials. Simon was a Zealot, an archenemy of Rome.

Matthew, on the other hand, was a collaborator with Rome. He was Jewish, but he accepted a position with the Roman government as a tax-collector. Most Americans are not fond of I.R.S. agents, but the tax collector was hated in Palestine. The Jews chafed under Roman taxation. The very idea that they had to pay taxes to Caesar galled them. Any Jew who would make a living helping the Romans collect taxes was despised as a traitor. To make matters worse, the tax collectors made their living by charging additional fees for their services. And most were rich. It was a system predisposed to corruption, accusation, and animosity. "Sinners and tax collectors" was an often-used phrase that suggested the two words were synonymous.

Matthew was a tax collector. Yet Jesus invited him to become one of his disciples. I wonder what was the first reaction of

Simon the Zealot when he asked Matthew, "What did you use to do for a living?" When Matthew said, "I was a tax-collector," the blood must have started to boil in Simon's veins. He must have thought of quitting the group immediately. Had he become too passive? Too liberal? Why, had he met Matthew in any other circle than this one, he may have slit the traitor's throat! But in the presence of Christ, the past differences were put to rest, and the Zealot and the tax-collector lived and worked together. The political lion lay down with the lamb. Amazing!

While Matthew and Simon had political differences, Thomas and Peter had personality differences. Thomas was a realist, probably a choleric personality. When Jesus couldn't be persuaded from going to Jerusalem, Thomas said, "Let us also go, that we may die with him" (John 11:16). When Jesus spoke in mystical language, Thomas spoke up and said, in effect, "Lord we don't understand what you're talking about!" (John 14:5). When the disciples insisted that Jesus had risen from the grave, Thomas refused to believe such an incredible claim without some tangible evidence. "Unless I see and touch for myself, I will not believe!" (John 20:25). Thomas was a thinker, a skeptic who wanted a solid intellectual reason for his belief and a good rationale for his behavior.

Simon Peter on the other hand was a dreamer, a 100% sanguine personality. Peter followed his emotions and spoke and reacted impulsively. When Jesus predicted he was going to die, Peter insisted it would never happen. He was a positive thinker! When Jesus appeared on the shore after his resurrection, Peter excitedly jumped overboard and swam ashore when he recognized Jesus. (Thomas was left to row the boat.) When Jesus came walking on water, it was Peter who got so enthusiastic that he said, "Lord, if that's you, invite me to come, and I'll walk on the water, too!" Thomas must have thought, "I can't believe he is actually going to try it!"

What a contrast in personality types. One emotional, the other cerebral. One sanguine, the other choleric. One gullible, the other skeptical. One vacillating, the other steady. One effervescent, the other somber. Don't you imagine that they got on each other's nerves sometimes? Can't you just hear Thomas muttering, "Come on, Peter, get in the real world!" And can't you hear Simon Peter complaining about Thomas' doubts? "When is he going to get with the program? He has no faith and no heart!" Yet, in the presence of Jesus Christ, these personality types were blended into a unit. The lion lay down with the lamb. Amazing!

The early church was a demonstration of God's eternal kingdom, too. The church was a place where formerly hostile groups lived at peace. Take Barnabas and Saul for example. Saul of Tarsus was a roaring lion. He went from house to house threatening and arresting Christians. He struck terror into the hearts of believers everywhere. Saul was ruthless and relentless in his determination to devour Christianity. When Saul was dramatically converted, he became a new creature. The lion became passive and loving. He repented of his past offenses and became zealous only to preach the cross of Christ.

But the Christians feared Saul. "When he came to Jerusalem, he tried to join the disciples, but they were all afraid of him, not believing that he really was a disciple" (Acts 9:26). But there was a wonderful Christian in Jerusalem by the name of Barnabas. Barnabas was a generous, compassionate, magnanimous Christian leader.

Barnabas befriended Saul. He listened to his conversion story and believed it. He introduced Saul to the church and encouraged the believers to extend fellowship and love to the former persecutor. Later, Barnabas and Saul joined together in a ministry in Antioch, and then again on a mission trip. The former persecutor of Christians and the Christian leader were unified. The lion had lain down with the lamb. It's amazing what the Prince of Peace can accomplish in the human heart!

Peter and Cornelius present another vivid example of how the early church brought peace to people who were formerly hostile. Peter was a staunch Jew, Cornelius a God-fearing Gentile. The Jews would not enter the home of a Gentile—much less eat with one. Even to touch a Gentile in the marketplace would render a Jew "unclean." Following his vision of the unclean beasts (see chapter 9), Peter entered Cornelius's, home, preached the gospel to him, and permitted him to be baptized without first becoming a Jew. That was a dramatic change in Peter's attitude. The wall separating the Hebrews from the Gentiles was broken down. The lion was lying down with the lamb.

Acts 13:1 reads, "In the church at Antioch there were prophets and teachers: Barnabas, Simeon called Niger, Lucius of Cyrene, Manaen (who had been brought up with Herod the Tetrarch) and Saul." That seemingly casual verse illustrates the incredible diversity that already existed in the early church.

There was a Jew (Barnabas) and a Gentile (Lucius of Cyrene), black (Niger was Latin for black) and white. There was the famous (Manaen, the foster brother of King Herod) and the obscure. The early church truly was a place where the barriers had broken down and formerly adversarial groups were living in harmony.

A Challenge to the Modern Church

The modern church should be a place where there can be unity in diversity. It should be a place where the lamb can lie down with the lion.

Jesus prayed that his followers would live at peace. "May they be brought to complete unity to let the world know that you sent me and have loved them even as you have loved me" (John 17:23).

We must understand that church fights, church splits, and denominational divisions are outside the will of God. We sometimes have to contend for the faith. But every time Christians fight with one another, it is a failure of the Spirit of God to prevail. It presents a horrible witness to the world.

Paul pleaded for the church to be at peace. "Make every effort to keep the unity of the Spirit through the bond of peace. There is one body and one Spirit—just as you were called to one hope when you were called" (Ephesians 4:3, 4).

The church should be a place where different *racial* groups can live in harmony. The rioting in Los Angeles that followed the Rodney King verdict illustrates the animosity that continues to fester between many blacks and whites. The government has been unable to solve the problem. What a challenge to the church to demonstrate that, in Christ, the racial barriers can be broken down. The lion can lie down with the lamb.

Following the L.A. riots, I met with the minister of a prominent black church in downtown Louisville. Three black youths in our city were on trial for mugging several whites. The trial had been well-publicized, and racial tension was mounting in our city. We needed to do something to defuse the potential for riots in Louisville.

We decided it would be healthy for our two churches to have a combined unity service as a testimony to the community that Christ can bring us together. We selected a Sunday night and rented the convention center downtown. Over 3000 people attended that service! The worship leaders from the two congregations took turns leading favorite songs and choruses, different singing groups shared their favorite style of music, and their minister and I both brought abbreviated sermons.

I mentioned that if we were going to spend eternity together, it seemed like a good idea to get acquainted on earth. The minister of the black church suggested it was time the church be "the headlight and not the taillight" in race relationships. We received a $15,000 offering for an inner city project. The spirit of that service was incredibly positive. Many stayed afterward and talked for a long time. Both groups admitted, "We've got some attitudes as Christians that need to be changed." We are now planning some future services and exchanges.

That unity service was the top story on the local TV stations and received front-page coverage in the paper the next day. The world was impressed that Christians were making an effort to be one in Christ. The lion and the lamb were worshiping as one.

In Christ "there is neither Jew nor Gentile, slave nor free, male nor female, for you are all one in Christ Jesus" (Galatians 3:28). The twentieth-century church should model harmony to a world filled with hostility.

The church should be a place where *denominational* barriers are breaking down. I grew up in a church that had a wonderful slogan: "We are not the only Christians, but we are Christians only." *Christian* was the only name that identified us, but we didn't claim to be God's only people. Unfortunately, that slogan often got buried under the same exclusive attitudes and superior spirits that exist in most denominations.

Respected Christian researcher George Barna states that his studies reveal a rapidly declining loyalty to denominations. People are looking for a church that stands for truth, meets personal needs and exalts Jesus Christ. The church that will have an impact for Christ in the twenty-first century will need to abandon sectarian spirits, leave room for differences of interpretations on secondary doctrines, and have fellowship with believers from a variety of backgrounds.

I have frequently attended the Praise Gathering, an interdenominational event sponsored by Bill and Gloria Gaither each year in Indianapolis. Twelve thousand people from across the country attend this three-day mini-revival just to worship Christ with thousands of other Christians. Bible-believing Christian people from dozens of backgrounds join together in exalting Christ in worship and studying God's Word in helpful sermons and Bible seminars. The worship styles differ, but

there is a common loyalty to Jesus Christ that binds those believers together. It's a tangible demonstration that God's people
are one.

When I played on the high-school basketball team my senior
year, my goal was to be the leading scorer in the county. The
top ten scorers were listed every week in the local paper, and
each week my name was among the top three. But there was
one problem: one of the others at the top of the list was a teammate of mine—Jim Komora. When we were winning games by
twenty-five points, I confess there were times when Jim shot
the ball and I secretly hoped he would miss! I wanted to be the
leading scorer. But when we played in the state tournament at
the end of the year, the games were all close. Then, when Jim
shot, I was praying that every shot would go in! The good of
the team had become more important than my selfish goals.

When a spirit of competition prevails between churches and
denominations, it indicates the people involved have their own
selfish interests at heart. When we begin to sense the awesome
spiritual battle that we face, we'll quit rooting against our own
teammates and "encourage one another—and all the more as
[we] see the Day approaching" (Hebrews 10:25).

The battle is not against those who honor Christ and his
Word. It is a "struggle . . . against the rulers, against the author-
ities, against the powers of this dark world and against spiritual forces of evil in the heavenly realms" (Ephesians 6:12). It's
imperative in this awesome spiritual conflict that God's people
be united and stand together.

The church should be a place where the barriers of *traditionalism* are broken down. There's a slogan that says, "Methods
are many; principles are few. Methods always change; principles never do." Failure to understand and apply that slogan has
created a lot of controversy and division among Christian people. Most church fights are not over doctrine, but over methods, music styles, worship structures, schedule changes, youth
programs, and the like. One church split over the addition of a
fellowship hall!

Many Christians have difficulty distinguishing between the
method and the message. They assume if there are new programs, new worship styles, new music, and changes in schedules, that the message is being altered. But methods have to
change because the culture changes, people age, previous
methods become threadbare, and the competition improves.
(Satan isn't using much flannel graph anymore. He's using

129

videos, strobe lights, sound bites, and rap music.) The church cannot stand pat on the methodology of twenty-five years ago. Will Rogers once said, "You can be on the right track and still get run over if you're standing still!"

Recently, when visiting my parents' home, I sat down and did something, I used to do every night before I went to bed. I hadn't done it in years. I ate a bowl of Wheaties. I sat at the same table where I grew up, eating cereal just before going to bed like I'd done hundreds of times as a boy. There was a sense of nostalgia as I sat there eating the cereal and reading the box. Same taste. Same size box. Same color. Same logo. Same slogan: "Breakfast of Champions." But there was one thing that was different. Mickey Mantle's picture wasn't on the front anymore. It was Michael Jordan. Same content, but different packaging. That's the reason General Mills continues to sell Wheaties after all these years.

Church leaders need to recognize and apply that principle. The content of the gospel must stay the same, but the packaging has to be altered from time to time. When this principle is properly understood and followed, there can be flexibility, tolerance, and harmony in spite of past tradition and personal preferences. The lamb of traditionalism can lie down with the lion of change.

The church should be a place where *individual hostilities* are broken down. Matthew and Simon, Peter and Thomas, Saul and Barnabas, Peter and Cornelius became unified in spite of individual differences. We can too. We must if the world is going to believe our message.

Bill and Joyce Molthop of our church were in a fairly serious accident one Memorial Day. A woman ran a stop sign and hit their car broadside. Both Bill and Joyce were taken to the hospital for emergency treatment of minor cuts and bruises. Later that day, the woman who caused the accident telephoned the Molthop home to inquire about their condition. Bill and Joyce's daughter Wendy answered. The woman said, "I feel so terrible about what's happened. I've been praying all day that your parents are okay." Even though the caller was a complete stranger, Wendy immediately sensed that she was a Christian because of her reference to prayer. Wendy responded, "I think they're okay, but don't blame yourself; accidents happen. Remember, the Bible says, 'All things work together for good.' This will too." There was no hostility, no angry accusation, no threat to sue. There was almost immediate harmony in a potentially volatile situation simply because of a common commitment to Christ. The lion of anger had lain down by the lamb of apology, and there was peace.

"Be kind and compassionate to one another, forgiving each other, just as in Christ God forgave you" (Ephesians 4:32).

A first-grade VBS teacher was a little uneasy when she saw that Davy, a boy who was visiting her class, had just one arm. She was concerned that the other children not make fun or make him feel awkward. Actually, the children did well and the evening went smoothly. But toward the end of the class, the teacher made a careless mistake. She said, 'Let's close the class with that little finger play. You know the one, "Here's the church, here's the steeple. Open the door and see all the people." No sooner were the words out of her mouth than she remembered Davy. Before she could correct the situation, a little girl sitting next to the disabled child reached her hand over and said, "Here, Davy; let's build the church together!"

If we're going to build the church of Jesus Christ in the twenty-first century, we'll have to be sensitive to each other's needs and cooperate fully. When the world sees the healthy helping the handicapped, the young assisting the old, the zealots embracing the tax collectors, and the lion lying down with the lamb, then maybe many will believe that Jesus is the Christ the Son of the living God—and the Prince of Peace.

CHAPTER 11

On Wings of Eagles

Deuteronomy 32:11

An eagle is one of the most impressive of all God's creatures. Anyone who has witnessed an eagle soaring overhead or through a canyon below is immediately impressed with its size. The wingspan of a mature eagle can measure up to eight feet across. It's one of the largest birds of prey.

More impressive than the eagle's size is its ability to fly. An eagle can attain speeds in excess of one hundred miles per hour in a dive! It often cruises at more than sixty miles per hour. Airplane pilots have reported seeing golden eagles in flight above 15,000 feet!

Gary Richmond in his book *All God's Creatures* reports that eagles court at these great heights. When they are ready to mate, the male locks talons with the female, and they free fall several thousand feet, mating as they fall. That's really falling in love! Eagles are one of the few species of animals that bond for life.[13]

Eagles are also noted for their keen eyesight. A human being has 200,000 visual receptors per square centimeter in his eyes; an eagle has 1.6 million receptors per square centimeter. That provides incredibly high visual resolution. If a person had the eyesight of an eagle, he could read three-inch high letters on a billboard a mile away! That sight serves the eagle well: an eagle can see a small fish jumping out of water five miles away. That's incredible!

An eagle is also noted for its impressive strength. A twenty-pound eagle has enough strength in its claws to break the

---

[13]Gary Richmond, *All God's Creatures*, p. 171.

bones in a man's forearm by merely grasping it firmly. God designed its powerful talons to pierce the flesh of a rabbit, fish, or small animal that the eagle has targeted. Richmond, a former veterinary assistant at the Los Angeles Zoo, reports that surgical needles were modified after eagles' talons.

> They are specially crafted to pierce flesh, not tear it. So we who have had to have cuts sutured or surgeries performed should be grateful for God having allowed us to recognize yet another useful application of His handiwork.[14]

The eagle's strength is enhanced by its coordination. Since the eagle can dive at over 100 miles per hour and all the while maintain its focus on the object of prey, it can hit its prey at that speed, sometimes with closed talons as if making a fist, and bash it unconscious or even kill it instantly. Eagles are so coordinated they can avoid midair collisions at high speed and actually drag just one eighth of an inch of talon across the back of another bird, sending it spiraling to the ground in shock.

No wonder the writer of Proverbs said that "the way of an eagle in the sky" was too amazing to understand (Proverbs 30:18, 19). No wonder our forefathers chose the bald eagle as the nation's symbol for independence. Everything about the eagle cries out for freedom and majesty. Richmond suggests that, while he sees a purpose for zoos' caging animals (to protect endangered species, to bring the wonders of the animal kingdom to the attention of mankind), "regal, noble, majestic eagles do not belong in cages."

> The Greek word for eagle is *aetos,* which means to blow as the wind or to become one with the wind. Animals who belong with the wind should not be expected to sit on perches all day and do nothing but look back at the people who look at them.[15]

Moses used the eagle to illustrate God's providential care for the nation of Israel. "You yourselves have seen what I did to Egypt and how I carried you on eagles' wings and brought you to myself" (Exodus 19:4). The Spirit of God is sometimes compared to a gentle dove, but in this passage, an eagle is used to

[14]Gary Richmond, *All God's Creatures,* p. 172.

[15]Gary Richmond, *All God's Creatures,* p. 170.

demonstrate how God delivered the Israelites from bondage. God is all-seeing and all-powerful. In His majesty, He is to be feared and respected. He alone can bring ultimate freedom from sin and death.

The Eagle Learns to Fly Through Struggle

One of the most intriguing passages about eagles describes the struggles of a young eagle learning to fly. The transition from being a helpless, baby bird in a nest to a majestic eagle soaring through the sky does not occur without fear and effort. Deuteronomy 32:11, 12 reads, "Like an eagle that stirs up its nest and hovers over its young, that spreads its wings to catch them and carries them on its pinions. The Lord alone led him." God compares his leading people to an eagle's teaching its young to fly.

The species mentioned in this passage may now be extinct. But we can well-imagine what a puzzling and difficult experience it was for this baby eagle to learn how to fly. It's helpful to understand that God develops maturity in us the same way.

First, the mother eagle stirs up the nest. She removes the rabbit's fur, the lamb's wool, and the soft leaves so that only the prickly briars remain. The once soft nest becomes a bed of discomfort. The baby eagles aren't cozy in their nest anymore. The mother wants them to be restless so they'll want to get out. Otherwise they'd be content to remain in the nest for a lifetime.

Sometimes God stirs up our nest, too. Changes take place in familiar surroundings that make us restless. A new supervisor, government interference, hostile neighbors, or a church fight can create discomfort in a setting where we were perfectly content a few weeks before. Sometimes we can't exactly put our finger on it, but we become dissatisfied and restless. Perhaps God is preparing us to move out of our comfort zone, into a deepening experience.

The mother eagle then hovers over its young. Perhaps she is demonstrating how to fly. More probably, she is refusing to feed them any longer. Instead of bringing food in her beak and settling down in the nest to protect them, she just hovers over them. She is deliberately creating hunger and increased dissatisfaction on the part of the young. They must desire to get out of that nest and learn to hunt for themselves. The mother's denial of basic needs would appear cruel and unfair to any who did not understand the ultimate goal—to produce mature eagles who can survive on their own.

Sometimes God does not provide for our simplest needs. We need a job, but the prayer is not instantly answered. We need someone to love, but no one is immediately available. We crave security and comfort, but our requests go unheeded. God seems unfair and unconcerned. If He is all-powerful, why would He refuse to supply such basic needs? Since we can't see the end result—spiritual maturity—God's rejection of our simple requests doesn't make much sense. God seems to be cruel and uncaring.

Then the mother eagle is described as "carrying her young on her pinions and spreading abroad her wings to catch them." What a spectacular sight it must have been for the writer to witness a mother eagle taking her baby on her back and soaring thousands of feet upward until she was just a tiny speck in the sky. The mother then did a surprising thing—she flipped over and the baby eagle was thrown off!

The baby eagle tumbles downward, wildly flapping its wings trying to learn to fly. The mother eagle glides downward, observing intently, and at the last moment she swoops under the falling infant and catches it on her back. She immediately starts climbing again, the baby eagle now clutching on for dear life! Can't you imagine that little eagle, eyes wild with fear saying, "Is this trip necessary?"

Once the mother has climbed thousands of feet, she once again flips over and the baby eagle goes awkwardly tumbling through the atmosphere again. This frightening process is repeated until the young eaglet learns how to fly on its own. Then the mother eagle considers her mission accomplished.

God Allows His People to Struggle

The Bible warns that the Christian life is going to have struggles. The Lord leads his people just as a mother eagle teaches her young to fly.

Some young believers naively assume that, if they live rightly, God will see to it that their lives are free from difficulty. The Scripture affirms just the opposite.

Jesus warned his followers repeatedly that God permits his people to go through struggles. "In the world you will have trouble" (John 16:33). "If they persecuted me they will persecute you" (John 15:20). "He causes his sun to rise on the evil and the good and sends rain to fall on the righteous and unrighteous" (Matthew 5:45). Peter said, "Dear friends, don't be surprised at the painful trial you are suffering, as though something strange were happening to you. But rejoice that you participate in the sufferings of Christ, so that you may be overjoyed when his glory is revealed" (1 Peter 4:12, 13).

The Lord could not make it any clearer. Christians are not exempt from cancer, financial disaster, a Downe's Syndrome baby, the death of a parent, automobile accidents, Parkinson's disease, the divorce of family members, or any other difficulty. The Christian life is not soaring to the heights without a struggle. Sometimes the bottom falls out and the believer finds himself tumbling downward, wondering where God's protection and providence come in.

In the ninth chapter of the Gospel of John is the story about a man who was healed of blindness. Jesus told him to go wash in the Pool of Siloam and he would be made well. He washed— and for the first time in his life he could see! He was exuberant. What a wonderful moment in this man's life! It seemed that all his troubles were over. Jesus had healed him.

But read further. In reality, his troubles had just begun. The enemies of Jesus began to harass him and his parents. He was questioned repeatedly. They challenged his theology. The Bible says, "They hurled insults at him." They kicked him out of the synagogue. Now that he could see, he had to get a job. His life was no longer a comfortable routine. Once he met Jesus, his blindness was cured, but his troubles had just started.

Have you ever talked with a starry-eyed young couple about to be married? Some are so eager. They can't wait to be married. "It's going to be so wonderful!" They can't think of anything better than to be with someone they love for the rest of their lives. If you are married, what do you tell them? You say, "Well—it's going to be good, but—there probably will be some difficulties, too. Don't be surprised when the romance fades. Hang in there."

I almost always tell them about an old minister who was married for over fifty years. He said sometimes he loved his wife so much he could just eat her up—and sometimes the next day he wished he had!

If one is going to mature through struggles, it is imperative that he anticipate them in advance and understand their purpose.

Connie Wurtenberger was a thirty-year-old mother of two boys and a woman of strong faith. During her pregnancy, she was excited about the birth of her third child. Two months before the baby was due, Connie discovered a lump on her neck and asked the doctor to examine it. A series of tests revealed that she had a cancer that had already spread to her lymph nodes. Her pregnancy prohibited X-rays to determine the origin of the malignancy. She was told that as soon as her baby was developed enough to live outside the womb, Connie would have to undergo chemotherapy.

What a blow for Connie! Just as she was soaring on top of the world, her world was flipped upside down, and she found herself tumbling through an experience she had not anticipated at all. Being a devout Christian did not exempt her from cancer at age thirty!

Connie asked the elders of our church to visit and pray for her healing. Her spirits were vibrant as she related to them that she had been a Christian since childhood, but now this tragic disease had driven her to prayer and an intense study of God's Word.

Connie said, "When I first learned how serious my cancer was, I asked, 'What have I done wrong that God would punish me in this way?' But then I was assured that God hadn't afflicted me, but that he would sustain me." She said, "God uses this kind of experience to deepen us. The Bible has become my arsenal. It's a place of weaponry and power. God has given me Scriptures for healing and strength. For example, I was reading about Daniel. It struck me that God didn't save Daniel *from* the lion's den but *through* it."

A few weeks later, a healthy baby was born to Connie and Jodi Wurtenberger. As of this writing, Connie is undergoing chemotherapy treatments and is making good progress. Her faith that God's keen eye is still watching and that God's everpresent love will still sustain her has been a source of inspiration to hundreds in our church.

The Bible makes it very clear that God will permit his people to undergo struggles to bring about maturity and to enhance our testimony. Paul said, "You know quite well that we were destined for them" (1 Thessalonians 3:3).

Acts 14:22 relates that Paul and Barnabas went from church to church "strengthening the disciples and encouraging them to remain true in their faith. 'We must go through many hardships to enter the kingdom of God,' they said." James wrote,

Consider it pure joy, my brothers, whenever [not *if* but *when*] you face trials of many kinds, because you know that the testing of your faith develops perseverance. Perseverance must finish its work so that you may be mature and complete, not lacking in anything (James 1:2-4).

Sheila Walsh wrote a book entitled *Holding on to Heaven with Hell on Your Back.* The Christian life has burdens. Satan wants to unsettle God's people. He wants to devour them. He brings trials today even as he did to Job, to try to crack the faith and destroy the testimony of each one.

There will come a time in every believer's life when life is tipped upside down, and the believer will find himself floundering for stability, grasping for something to prevent him from smashing against the rocks of disillusionment below. It's important in such times to remember God's promises, "The Lord your God . . . will never leave you nor forsake you" (Deuteronomy 31:6). "God is faithful; he will not let you be tempted beyond what you can bear. But when you are tempted, he will also provide a way out so that you can stand up under it" (1 Corinthians 10:13).

Our Reaction to Struggle

Tim Hansel was seriously injured in a mountain climbing accident years ago. He now lives every day with severe back pain. In spite of daily adversity, he wrote a book entitled *You Gotta' Keep Dancin'* in which he relates the importance of joy in the Christian life. Tim makes this memorable statement to summarize the final point of this chapter; "Suffering is inevitable, but misery is optional."

God is going to allow us to suffer. We can't control that. But we can control our response to suffering. We can control our attitude. There are basically five ways to respond to struggles.

We Can Respond Irrationally

A group of Boy Scouts from the city was camping in the woods by the river, where they were eaten alive by mosquitoes! The mosquitoes were so fierce the boys tried to hide under blankets to escape. One of them peeked out and saw lightning bugs all around the camp. He called to his buddies, "We might as well give up. They're coming at us with flashlights!"

When faced with adversity, some will almost always exaggerate the problem and respond irrationally. "The people in Canaan are giants. We're like grasshoppers in their sight!" complained the ten negative spies. One can be so afraid or so hurt as to lose all sense of reason. He goes into seclusion, or she considers running away, dropping out of church—or even suicide. When Elijah was under pressure from Jezebel, he said, "God take my life, I'm the only prophet left in Israel." God responded, "That's not true, Elijah. There are 7000 prophets who are faithful." Elijah had reacted irrationally to his struggle. (See 1 Kings 19:9-18.)

We Can React Resentfully

When Job's wife lost her wealth, her ten children were killed, and her husband's health was broken, she said, "Curse God and die!" Some people get very angry at God and become extremely bitter about life. "If there were a loving, powerful God, he wouldn't let this happen to me," they fume.

Someone said, "Realism is idealism that has been through the fire and been purified. Cynicism is idealism that has been through the fire and got burned." Whether you get purified or burned doesn't depend on the intensity of the fire, but the tenacity of your spirit.

Some Respond to Struggle Passively

"Que sera, sera" the old slogan goes. That summarizes the response of the stoic. "Whatever will be will be." If something good happens, don't get too excited; if something bad happens, don't get depressed. Like a turtle who takes the prodding of a stick, there are those who withdraw into a shell and refuse to demonstrate any emotional response to trouble.

There's an old legend about a Chinaman whose horse broke out of the coral and ran away. His neighbors sympathized, "Sorry to hear about your horse—too bad."

"Well, we don't know if it's bad or not," said the Chinaman. "Wait and see." The next day the horse returned and led five beautiful wild stallions into the fold.

"Good news about your horse returning," the neighbors said.

"Well, we don't know if it's good news or not," said the Chinaman.

The next week his son was kicked off one of the wild stallions and the boy broke his leg. "So sorry about you son," said the neighbors. "Too bad he broke his leg."

"Well, we're not sure it's all bad," responded the Chinaman.

The next day a military leader came by conscripting all able-bodied young men for the military. The Chinaman's son was exempted because of his disability and all the neighbors rejoiced, "Good news about your son's not having to go off to war," they said.

But the Chinaman said, "We can't be sure it's good news or not."

A week later the young soldiers returned from a victorious battle and celebrated by dividing up the spoils among them. "Too bad your son was not able to go with us," one of them said.

"We're not sure that's bad," said the Chinaman.

That story could go on forever! What appears to be good news one day is bad the next and vice-versa. As a result, some take a stoic approach to life and try to take the good and the bad in stride. Don't get too excited, don't get depressed. Whatever will be will be. That may be a better reaction than irrationality or resentment, but it's not the best reaction.

We Can Respond Faithfully

When Job experienced all his tragedies, he refused to curse God and die. He said, "Shall I receive good at the hand of God and not evil?" "Though he slay me, still I will trust him."

The faithful Christian admits, "I don't know why God has allowed this difficulty in my life, but I still believe he exists. I still believe he loves and watches over me. I still believe that 'in all things God works for the good of those who love him' (Romans 8:28). I hold on to my faith with my fingernails, but I hold on."

Revelation 2:10 reads,

> Do not be afraid of what you are about to suffer. I tell you, the devil will put some of you in prison to test you, and you will suffer persecution for ten days. Be faithful, even to the point of death, and I will give you the crown of life.

Robert Schuller has written a book with a great title: *Life Is Unfair, but God Is Good.* He says people mistake the facts of life with the acts of God. God is not unfair. Life is unfair. God is faithful. God is good.

The Christian must remain faithful in spite of difficulty. And yet, there is one more—a better—response than just hanging on to faith.

We Can Use Trouble Creatively

The eaglet is allowed to struggle for a purpose. He does not struggle just so he will trust the mother. He struggles to learn

141

to fly! God's allowing us to struggle is for a purpose as well—to bring about maturity, to enhance our testimony, and to increase our abilities.

Woody Stephens was disappointed that he didn't grow to be normal size. But he loved horses, and he became a jockey and then a famous trainer. Jay Leno has one of the most pointed chins I've ever seen, but he's used that oddity creatively and has become a well-known comedian. Mel Tillis stutters terribly. But instead of wallowing in self-pity, he laughs about it and endears himself to millions of fans. I read somewhere that high heels were invented by a woman who got tired of having her boyfriend kiss her on the forehead!

People who learn to use difficulty creatively are impressive. God's people should look for opportunities to use their difficulties for the better. When Paul was imprisoned, he was disappointed. But he did more than just faithfully trust God to deliver him. Paul took advantage of the opportunity by writing letters and witnessing to prison guards. He wrote from prison, "I want you to know, brothers, that what has happened to me has really served to advance the gospel. As a result it has become clear throughout the whole palace guard and to everyone else that I am in chains for Christ" (Philippians 1:12, 13).

When people are bitter about their trials, it's discouraging. But there are few things more inspirational than a Christian who responds faithfully and creatively in spite of trials. Fanny Crosby was blind. Instead of wallowing in self-pity, she wrote hymns that the church has sung for decades. "To God Be the Glory," "Tell Me the Story of Jesus," "Jesus is Calling," "Blessed Assurance," "I Am Thine, O Lord," and many more. When she was very old, someone told her that if she had been born at that time in history, an operation could have been performed that would have given her sight. She said, "I wouldn't change a thing—do you realize the very first thing I'll ever be able to see is the face of Jesus?" Fanny Crosby's struggle had brought about a spiritual maturity that few others have achieved.

Dave Reavor was critically injured in the Viet Nam war. A grenade explosion tore off half his face, one arm, and several fingers on the other hand. Amazingly, his life was spared, but his body was permanently mutilated. Plastic surgery has improved his appearance, but he is still the object of cruel stares and name calling. But Dave Reavor has used his grotesque appearance to give a positive testimony about how Christ is able to sustain through incredible difficulty. A keen sense of humor enables Dave to poke fun at his handicaps, and his audiences find themselves laughing with him one moment and weeping with him the next. He reaches hundreds for Christ every year. Instead of throwing a "Pity party," Dave Reavor learned to fly from falling.

Several years ago, I heard a man named Dave Ring speak. I was at a conference and some of the best-known speakers and authors had already spoken to the assembly. I had never heard Ring speak before, and I wondered why he was on the program—until he began to speak.

David Ring was born with cerebral palsy. He has such a heavy speech impediment that his listeners have to struggle to understand him. People who hear only his voice and not his words no doubt wonder why this man so handicapped is asked to speak at conferences that feature nationally known speakers and authors. But David Ring held that audience of 12,000 spellbound for twenty minutes as he talked about what it was like to grow up so attached to his "mama" and then to see her die. But he said God was good and God had sustained him through grief.

Then he slurred, "They said I woul' neber ride a bike—but I did! They said I woul' neber get marwied—but I did! And I got fibe kids to pwoove it!" (Of course the audience burst into laughter.) Then he added, "They said I woul' neber be able to pweach, but this pas' year I pweached 265 times! . . . Now, I got cewebwal palsy, yet I pweach—what's your pwobwem?"

I had heard some of the finest preachers in the nation that week and never shed a tear. But as I sat there in the darkness of that auditorium, tears rolled down my cheeks. What God didn't do through famous authors and big-name preachers, he did for me through a man with cerebral palsy who used his struggles creatively.

Paul said, "God chose the foolish things of the world to shame the wise; God chose the weak things of this world to shame the strong. He chose the lowly things of this world and the despised things . . . . . to nullify the things that are, so that no one may boast before him" (1 Corinthians 1:27-29). When you are at your lowest, weakest moment, that may be the time God uses you to make the greatest impact. Like the eagle, when you are falling, it may be when you are about to learn to fly.

John Claypool ministered at the Crescent Hill Baptist Church in Louisville, Kentucky, for a number of years. During that ministry, his young daughter was diagnosed with leukemia.

For a period she went into remission and seemed perfectly normal. Her family was in hopes that the diagnosis had been incorrect or that she had experienced the miracle of divine healing for which John and so many had been praying.

In his book, *Tracks of a Fellow Struggler,* Dr. Claypool related that those hopes came to an abrupt end, ironically one Easter Sunday morning. The old pains reappeared, and his little girl went into a severe relapse that involved hospitalization for two weeks. Part of the time both of her eyes were swollen shut, and every part of her body was racked with pain.

John Claypool reported that moving with her through those two weeks was an unspeakably draining experience. He found himself stretched in every way—physically exhausted, emotionally dissipated, spiritually challenged—as never before.

The worst moment came one night when his daughter could get no relief, and she asked him, "Daddy, when will this leukemia go away?"

He answered, "We don't know, darling, but we're doing everything in our power to find an answer and cure it. "

There was a long silence, and then she asked, "Have you asked God when the leukemia will go away?"

Her pastor/father, choked back the tears and sobbed, "You know, darling, how we have prayed again and again for God to help us."

But she persisted, "Have you asked God when it will go away—what did He say? "

Claypool asked, "How do you respond to such a childlike directness at a time when the heavens seem utterly silent?" There are times when there are no immediate answers.

A few hours later, John Claypool's daughter died. In spite of his heavy heart, he decided to preach the next Sunday. That message, recorded for posterity, was one of the most moving sermons I've ever heard. It was based on Isaiah 40:31, "Those who hope in the Lord will renew their strength. They will soar on wings like eagles; they will run and not grow weary, they will walk and not be faint."

Dr. Claypool said, "There are three stages of life represented in that passage. Sometimes we mount up with wings as an eagle and fly. We're on top of the world. Sometimes we run and don't grow weary. We perform the routine. But there are times when it's all we can do to walk and not faint. That's where I am today. I'm barely holding on to my faith. I need your prayers and assistance."

At that moment when Dr. John Claypool was at his lowest, he preached his most powerful sermon! Perhaps his greatest contribution to God's kingdom came during his darkest hour— and he wasn't even aware of it. But because he faced a severe trial faithfully and creatively, God used him to buoy up others for years to come. Paul said, "[God's] power is made perfect in weakness. . . . For when I am weak, then I am strong" (2 Corinthians 12:9, 10).

Any time you think life is unfair, look at the cross. It wasn't fair for the perfect Son of God to be nailed to that tree at age thirty-three. It wasn't fair for him to suffer pain, ridicule, guilt, loneliness and death.

It seemed on that dark day that the world had turned upside down, and God's people were falling into despair. But three days later, Jesus Christ arose from the grave to live in triumph. He has promised, if we walk in faith, he will do the same for us. That's the reason we can walk and not faint. That's the reason we can smile even through tears. We know there will come a day when we shall rise up again with eagles. And fly!

CHAPTER 12

The Value of Work

Proverbs 6:6-11

O ne usually thinks of ants as a nuisance. No homemaker welcomes an ant in the house. Ants are a pest to fruit-growers and Public Enemy Number One to picnickers.

But some insect-eating ants are considered beneficial. In the American tropics, army ants are welcomed as highly efficient insect exterminators. The temporary inconvenience caused by the intrusion of a colony of army ants into a house is out-weighed by the fact that, when the ants leave, the house will be free of insects.

In the book of Proverbs ants are used to teach a positive les-son. "Go to the ant, you sluggard, consider its ways and be wise" (Proverbs 6:6) Just what positive lessons can God's peo-ple learn from ants?

Ants Provide an Indictment of the Lazy Man

According to the *Encyclopedia Britannica,* there are more than 5000 known species of ants, including the 600 species and sub-species that live in the United States. Their habits vary signifi-cantly. Most ants nest in the ground, but others have an ability to utilize a wide variety of nest sites. In some species, the queen ant is winged at maturity, for mating purposes, but other queen ants have no wings. Ants differ in size, color, and food prefer-ence.

In spite of their variety, ants have one thing in common. They are workers! Ants are instinctively diligent creatures. Whether it is scouting out food at a picnic, carting a morsel back to the anthill, burrowing in the ground, feeding the larvae, protecting the queen, or fighting battles against adversaries, the ant is constantly active.

In Proverbs 6, the ambitious ant provides an indictment of the sluggard who refuses to do his share of work. I read recently about an award given to the world's laziest man: he whittles with an electric knife! That's lazy!

God is not pleased with the man or woman who is lazy. Genesis introduces us to a God who works. For six days God labored, creating the universe. Genesis 2:2 relates that, on the seventh day, God finished his work and rested. God was not tired and needing a break, but there was a temporary change of pace in his activity. God is at work today sustaining his creation, restraining evil, and saving man. Jesus said, "My Father is always at his work to this very day, and I, too, am working" (John 5:17).

God created man to share in his work. Some of my fonder memories of my boyhood days are of times my dad and I worked together putting up fence posts, weeding in the garden, or baling hay. I sometimes protested, but there is something about working together that enhances relationships. God created man for fellowship with him. "The Lord God took the man and put him in the Garden of Eden to work it and take care of it" (Genesis 2:15). God planted the garden, and man was to cultivate it. They shared in the work.

The Bible makes it clear that God considers laziness a sin—a rejection of his offer of fellowship. "The sluggard is wiser in his own eyes than seven men who answer discreetly" (Proverbs 26:16). "Lazy hands make a man poor, but diligent hands bring wealth. He who gathers crops in summer is a wise son, but he who sleeps during harvest is a disgraceful son" (Proverbs 10:4, 5) The one-talent man who buried his talent and refused to work was called a "wicked, lazy servant," by Jesus (Matthew 25:26). We don't call lazy people wicked today, we say they "have a low leisure level!" But Paul said, "If a man will not work, he shall not eat" (2 Thessalonians 3:10).

The book of Proverbs suggests four characteristics of a lazy man. Each one is a trait that ought to be avoided because of the harmful consequences associated with it.

He Can't Get Started in the Morning

"How long will you lie there, you sluggard? When will you get up from your sleep? A little sleep, a little slumber, a little folding of the hands to rest—and poverty will come on you like a bandit" (Proverbs 6:9-11). The lazy student is always late to first-hour class. Every morning it's a battle to get out of bed. He goes to church at St. Mattress on Sunday morning. He can sleep till noon without a twinge of conscience. "As a door turns on its hinges, so a sluggard turns on his bed" (Proverbs 26:14). He rolls over to turn off the snooze alarm again and again. "Do not love sleep or you will grow poor. Stay awake and you will have food to spare" (Proverbs 20:13).

He Seldom Finishes Anything

"The lazy man does not roast his game, but the diligent man prizes his possessions" (Proverbs 12:27) The sluggard enjoys the hunt—that's the fun part. But he doesn't want to clean and roast the game. That's the tedious part. One of the characteristics of a lazy person is the failure to complete projects. He's got a lot of good ideas and good intentions, but the basement is full of unfinished projects, There just wasn't enough discipline to finish. "If a man is lazy, the rafters sag; if his hands are idle, the house leaks" (Ecclesiastes 10:18).

He Is Full of Excuses

This is a third characteristic of a lazy man: he has an excuse for everything! "The sluggard says, 'There is a lion outside!' or, 'I will be murdered in the streets!'" (Proverbs 22:13). There is always some excuse not to work.
"It's a jungle out there!"
"It's Friday and everyone takes off Friday afternoon."
"It's Monday and no one buys on Monday."
"It's too hot."
"It's too cold."
"I've got to be careful not to burn out."
"There's a recession, so there's no use trying now."
"I need to spend time with my nephew."
"I need to stay home today and rearrange my sock drawer."
The sluggard can find a hundred excuses not to work. He seldom says, "I don't *feel* like working today, but I'm going to do it anyway."

He Appears to Get Bad Breaks

It seems that one thing after another goes wrong. The car breaks down at the most inopportune time. The competition comes up with a new product just before the sale was to be closed. The electricity went off during the night and the alarm was off.

"The way of the sluggard is blocked with thorns, but the path of the upright is a highway" (Proverbs 15:19). In other words, you make your own breaks. It's amazing how many times good "luck" comes to those who work. The lazy man thinks that his failure is due to bad breaks; in reality, his own lethargy has blocked the path. "The sluggard does not plow in season; so at harvest time he looks but finds nothing" (Proverbs 20:4).

"Go to the ant, you sluggard; consider its ways and be wise!" (Proverbs 6:6). The ambitious ant incriminates the lazy man.

The Ant Provides an Incentive for the Laboring Man

In his observation of ant colonies, Solomon was impressed that these tiny creatures apparently worked instinctively and voluntarily. "It has no commander, overseer or ruler, yet it stores its provisions in summer and gathers its food at harvest" (Proverbs 6:7, 8). God designed the ant with an instinct for work.

Many people regard work as a curse. They envision God screaming angrily at Adam and Eve, "You have sinned! There's only one fitting punishment for your disobedience. You will have to work every day for the rest of your lives!"

But that's not true. Adam and Eve were given work to do before they sinned. "The Lord God took the man and put him in the Garden of Eden to work it and take care of it" (Genesis 2:15). Adam was given the responsibility of cultivating the garden before he sinned. Work was a part of his perfect existence.

The curse was not work, but that work would be painful and difficult. "Cursed is the ground because of you; through painful toil you will eat of it all the days of your life. It will produce thorns and thistles for you. . . . By the sweat of your brow you will eat your food" (Genesis 3:17-19). It was not work that was a curse—it was yard work!

Partners With God

When we work at legitimate labor, we are partners with God in providing for the needs of the world. A deacon showed the new preacher around his immaculate farm. The preacher was impressed with the plush pasture surrounded by a beautiful white fence. He said, "The Lord sure has a beautiful pasture here." When the minister saw the scenic man-made lake, he said, "The Lord certainly has a lovely lake there." He looked at the wheat and corn fields and said, "The Lord has a good crop growing there." Finally, the exasperated farmer said, "Preacher, you should have seen this place when the Lord had it all to himself!"

Adam and Eve worked as partners with God to take care of the garden. When we work at legitimate labor, we are co-laborers with God in providing for his world.

Exodus 35 contains God's instructions for the building of the tabernacle.

> Then Moses said to the Israelites, "See the Lord has chosen Bezalel . . . to make artistic designs for work in gold, silver and bronze, to cut and set stones, to work in wood and engage in all kinds of artistic craftsmanship. And he has given both him and Oholiab . . . the ability to teach others. He has filled them with skill to do all kinds of work as craftsmen and designers, embroiderers in blue, purple and scarlet yarn and fine linen, and weavers, all of them master craftsmen and designers. . . to do the work just as the Lord commanded" (Exodus 35:30–36:1).

Their work as designers, embroiderers, color experts, and teachers was ordained of God. They were just as called as the priests were. They were partners with God in constructing the tabernacle.

There are 220 different occupations mentioned in the Bible, and each one is a partnership with God. A schoolteacher is a partner with God in preparing young people for life. It is God's will that a child matures intellectually. When a teacher plans lessons, instructs and disciplines students, grades tests, she is a partner with God in developing his children.

A nurse is a partner with God in helping to restore his people to health or to alleviate discomfort. Artists, musicians, and entertainers are partners with God, using their gifts to enhance the quality of people's lives.

Doug Sherman and William Hendrix have written a helpful book entitled *Your Work Matters to God.* In it they write,

> We think your work matters deeply to God. . . . Work is not something we do apart from God, as the secular world would view it. Work is not something beneath God's dignity and concern, as [some Christians] view it. . . . Work is a major part of human life that God takes very seriously. . . . [It] has intrinsic value. Through work we serve people, meet our own needs, meet our family's

needs, earn money to give to others; and through work we love God.[16]

It is easy to see how a psychologist, social worker, doctor, or mother helps people and serves God through his or her occupation. But what about a cashier, a data processor, an actuary, a C.P.A., or an I.R.S. agent? How do their jobs contribute to what God wants done in the world? It may not be obvious, but a little thought will reveal how every legitimate occupation is a partnership with God in meeting the world's needs. Hendrix cites an example that illustrates this point.

He tells about a man who owned a pallet company. Pallets are the wooden platforms used extensively in the transportation industry to make it easier for forklifts to load and unload stacks of goods. How could that man's pallets possibly contribute to the work of God in the world?

Those pallets are an indispensable part of the trucking industry, an industry that delivers grapefruit from Texas, cereal from Michigan, and milk from Ohio to the supermarket near your home, says Hendrix. All that comes together at your breakfast table. Before you eat, you give thanks to God. Why? Because he provided the food. But he used a system of workers to bring that food: farmers who raised it, scientists who checked it for purity, farm equipment dealers who sold the machinery, bankers who arranged financing, truck drivers, service station operators, construction workers (who laid the highway), supermarket employees—On and on it goes! But included in that list of people who provided breakfast is the pallet manufacturer!

Meeting the needs of families is something God wants done. The man who manufactures pallets is contributing to the work of God in the world. It is important to realize that God uses our work even if no one ever says, "I thank God for what you are doing."

Once we grasp this concept, it revolutionizes our attitude toward work. We are not performing a task just to draw a paycheck or to please an employer, but to serve God and our fellowman. Then it is much easier to be like an ant, working hard without being pushed by an overseer or ruler.

---

[16]Doug Sherman and William Hendrix, *Your Work Matters to God* (Colorado Springs: NavPress, 1987), selected excerpts. Used by permission.

While traveling one summer, I saw a huge sign over a place of business that read,

"H. & S. FARM EQUIPMENT COMPANY
TO GOD BE THE GLORY."

The owner understood that his work was God's work. The apostle Paul agrees:

Whatever you do, work at it with all your heart, as working for the Lord, not for men, since you know that you will receive an inheritance from the Lord as a reward. It is the Lord Christ you are serving (Colossians 3:23, 24).

You go to work for the very same reason you to go church—to worship and serve Christ.

It's important to understand, in this discussion, that our work must be legitimate work to honor God. Obviously, if a person is working as a prostitute, a thief, a hit man, or a drug-dealer, that person is involved in a work that God does not want done in the world. Such a one certainly is not a partner with God.

Each job needs to be performed for God's glory. There may be some gray areas, but if you conclude you are involved in work that is contrary to God's will, then begin to look for a way out. Don't spend your life in a vocation that is not a partnership with God.

It's also important to understand that every legitimate job is a high calling. Sometimes Christian leaders have left the impression that the highest calling is to be an ordained minister or a missionary. One minister testified, "I was working as an engineer, designing bridges. Then one day I realized, 'God is going to burn all these bridges up someday. What significance is there in designing bridges? I want to be involved in something that lasts for eternity.' So I quit designing bridges, and I'm now a full-time minister in God's service."

The disturbing implication is that a design engineer is, at best, a second-rate Christian. If a Christian were really dedicated, he would quit his secular employment and become involved in "eternal matters." But God doesn't have a two-tiered scale of service. He does call some into paid ministries. But God also equips some to design bridges so that the evangelist doesn't fall through and kill himself on the way to church! God gifts some to build bridges and make money and be generous so the minister can have a car to drive to the hospital. The engineer who designs bridges to the glory of God is just as important in God's perspective as the minister who preaches sermons.

Daniel was a statesman. Joseph was an administrator. Gideon was a soldier. David a musician, shepherd, song writer, soldier, and politician. Jesus worked for over a decade as a carpenter. When it came time to choose disciples, he did not choose the cream of the crop from among the Pharisees. He called men from the marketplace who would never have been mistaken as religious leaders.

If teachers don't teach, we'll have illiteracy. If farmers don't harvest, we'll have starvation. If scientists don't research, we'll have disease. If policemen don't parole, we'll have anarchy. If salesmen don't sell, we'll have a stagnant economy. That's the reason Paul said, "Whatever you do . . . it is the Lord Christ you are serving" (Colossians 3:23, 24). Our daily jobs are partnerships with God in meeting the needs of his world.

Character Development

God uses our work to develop character in us. The proverb doesn't say, "Consider the ant and be rich," but, "Consider the ant and be wise." Riches may come to those who work hard, but God is much more concerned about our character than he is about our comfort.

God develops character through difficulty. James said,

> Consider it pure joy, my brothers, whenever you face trials of many kinds, because you know that the testing of your faith develops perseverance. Perseverance must finish its work so that you may be mature and complete, not lacking anything (James 1:2-4).

Maybe you have a job that is a trial. Your employer makes life miserable with his demands. Your co-workers make you uncomfortable with their un-Christian life-style and language. Your responsibilities are so mundane that you just tolerate your job because nothing better is available. Your pay is so meager that you barely survive.

You may fantasize about what it would be like to be in a different job. You think, "It would be so wonderful to work in church with Christians who are honest and dependable." Or you say, "I would love to own my own business where I could set my own agenda and not have a boss on my back." Perhaps you are praying that God would remove you from your unful-filling job.

But maybe you are exactly where the Lord wants you to be. Maybe your job is a classroom for learning character. He's using your boss as "Heavenly sandpaper" to smooth out the rough edges of your life. He's using your job as a crucible to develop maturity in you. There are qualities you can learn at work that you won't learn anywhere else—honesty, depend-ability, loyalty, sensitivity, patience, self-control, enthusiasm, flexibility, persistence, cheerfulness, integrity, confidence, for-giveness, punctuality.

James suggests that instead of moping around, feeling sorry for yourself at work, you ought to "count it all joy." The next time your boss gives you a hard time, go to him with a smile and say, "Thanks! God is really using you to develop my char-acter!" I'm sure he will be impressed!

Obedience to God is often learned through a process that is no fun at the time. But the most important thing you bring home from work is not your paycheck—it's your character.

God develops character through responsibility. Maybe you love your job, it challenges and excites you. You are making good money. Maybe you even feel guilty sometimes that things are going so well. God sometimes develops character through opportunity and responsibility. Thomas Carlyle once said, "For every man who can withstand prosperity, I'll find you a hun-dred who can withstand adversity." Prosperity is a test of char-acter, too.

Jesus told about a merchant who was given five talents of money. He didn't give it all away and enter a monastery. He put the talents to work. He invested it wisely. When the owner called for an accounting of the trust, the steward said, "Here are the five talents you entrusted to me; I have earned five more." The owner didn't respond, "You greedy, self-centered servant. How could you accumulate more when there was a man with only one talent next to you?" No, the owner said, "Well done good and faithful servant. Enter into your master's happiness."

The man with five talents had taken advantage of the oppor-tunity. The Lord was pleased that he had worked to increase his resources and enhance his character.

One Christian businessman explained why he invests in restaurants and fast food shops. "I like to take a raw piece of land and make it productive. The store or restaurant I put up sells food and other items that people need. It provides income for the employees I hire. It also gives me a good return on my investment."

God wants people to have food, jobs, and necessities. He also wants an investor to get a fair return on his investment. That man is a partner with God in providing for needs, and he's also developing character in his own life.

If your job has a ton of opportunity, put your hand to the task and do it well. Work diligently. Treat others with integrity. Give generously. Then God is honored and your character is matured.

Self Esteem

God wants us to work to enhance our self-esteem, "That everyone may eat and drink, and find satisfaction in all his toil— this is the gift of God" (Ecclesiastes 3:13).

"Do you see a man skilled in his work? He will serve before kings; he will not serve before obscure men" (Proverbs 22:29). That doesn't mean that every skilled worker will be called to the White House. But there is a sense of honor and dignity that results from legitimate work.

When I get depressed, I can usually trace it to one of two causes: either my feelings have been hurt, or I feel guilty because I haven't worked as hard as I think I should. Nothing gets me out of depression quicker than putting my hand to a task and getting something accomplished.

God created us with certain emotional needs that are going to be met only by an honest day's work. There is a sense of accomplishment and self-respect that can only come from the satisfaction of a job well-done.

I remember my first job. I worked in a nursery hoeing weeds from around seedlings. It was a tedious job for eight hours a day—and for just 80 cents an hour! The first day I thought, "I can't do this all day!" But I also remember standing at the end of a row of tiny pine trees and looking back at the clean, cultivated seedlings and thinking to myself, "That looks great! Good job!" When I went home that night, I was exhausted, but there was a wonderful feeling of accomplishment, too. That experience began to build self-respect.

In his book, *Christians in the Marketplace*, Bill Hybels wrote,

Dignity is available to every person in every legitimate profession. ...The farmer who plows a straight furrow, the accountant whose books balance, the truck driver who backs a forty foot rig into a narrow loading dock, the teacher who delivers a well-prepared lesson, the carpenter who keeps the building square, the executive who reads the market accurately, the factory worker who labors with speed and accuracy, the secretary who types the pages perfectly, the student who masters a foreign language, the athlete who plays the game aggressively, the mother who tends her children faithfully, the minister who prepares his sermon and preaches it powerfully, all experience dignity as they commit themselves to their labors.[17]

I have a plaque in my office that contains this quote from Vince Lombardi, the legendary coach of the Green Bay Packers. "I firmly believe that man's finest hour, his greatest fulfillment to all he holds dear, is that moment when he has worked his heart out in a good cause and lies exhausted on the field of battle, victorious."

That's the reason some people get discouraged when they retire. They have lost their sense of purpose, and their self-esteem takes a nose dive. Some people who inherit money and have no need of working become extremely dissatisfied.

I know of a man who sold his business and made millions. Within three months, he had bought an auto repair shop. He said, "I have to do something. I don't need the money, but I need the work." People are happiest when they are accomplishing something worthwhile.

My son Phil loves to produce videos for various organizations. He recently finished one for the recreation department of our church. When he was finished interviewing, splicing, superimposing titles, adding background music, and condensing it to the right time frame, he brought it home, called his mother and me into the room and said, "Watch this. What do you think?" It's a joy to see his self-confidence enhanced by doing a tedious job well.

When we train our children to work we are enhancing their self-esteem and preparing them for eternity. If you think Heaven is a place of eternal rest, you're going to be disappointed. The Bible informs us there will be responsibility, service, and work in Heaven. "No longer will there be any more curse. The throne of God and of the Lamb will be in the city,

---

[17]Bill Hybels, *Christians in the Marketplace* (Wheaton: Victor Books, a division of Scripture Press, 1982). Used by permission.

and his servants will serve him" (Revelation 22:3). Instead of eternal bliss, there will be service, responsibility, work, and a challenge to grow and achieve.

The movie *Chariots of Fire* tells the story of Eric Liddell, an Olympic runner from Scotland in the 1920s. Eric's sister questioned why he intended to run in the Olympics rather than enter the ministry. In a very dramatic moment, he turned to her and said, "Jenny, God made me for a purpose—for China. But he also made me fast. When I run, I feel his pleasure. It's not just fun. To win is to honor him!" Eric Liddell recognized that God wanted to use his testimony in the Olympics. When you go to your place of employment, he wants you to feel his presence and his pleasure.

"Whatever you do, work at it with all your heart, as working for the Lord, not for men, since you know that you will receive an inheritance from the Lord as a reward. It is the Lord Christ you are serving."